FOIL PACK
DINNERS

— ✕ —

FOIL PACK DINNERS

×

100 DELICIOUS, QUICK-PREP RECIPES FOR THE GRILL AND OVEN

JULIA RUTLAND

TILLER PRESS

NEW YORK LONDON TORONTO SYDNEY NEW DELHI

TILLER PRESS

An Imprint of Simon & Schuster, Inc.
1230 Avenue of the Americas
New York, NY 10020

First Tiller Press trade paperback edition May 2020

TILLER PRESS and colophon are trademarks of Simon & Schuster, Inc.

For information about special discounts for bulk purchases,
please contact Simon & Schuster Special Sales at 1-866-506-1949
or business@simonandschuster.com.

The Simon & Schuster Speakers Bureau can bring authors to your live event.
For more information or to book an event, contact the Simon & Schuster Speakers
Bureau at 1-866-248-3049 or visit our website at www.simonspeakers.com.

Interior design by Matt Ryan
Photography produced by Blueline Creative Group LLC.
Visit www.bluelinecreativegroup.com
Produced by Katherine Cobbs
Photography by Liam Franklin
Food Stylist: Margaret Monroe Dickey
Prop styling by Claire Spollen, Margaret Monroe Dickey, Katherine Cobbs
Food Stylist Assistant: Kady Wohlfarth

Manufactured in the United States of America

1   3   5   7   9   10   8   6   4   2

Library of Congress Cataloging-in-Publication Data

Names: Rutland, Julia Dowling, author.
Title: Foil pack dinners : 100 delicious, quick-prep recipes
for the grill and oven / by Julia Rutland.
Identifiers: LCCN 2019056190 (print) | LCCN 2019056191 (ebook) |
ISBN 9781982141080 (paperback) | ISBN 9781982141097 (ebook)
Subjects: LCSH: Dinners and dining. | Aluminum foil. |
Quick and easy cooking. | LCGFT: Cookbooks.
Classification: LCC TX737 .R88 2020 (print) | LCC TX737 (ebook) | DDC 642—dc23
LC record available at https://lccn.loc.gov/2019056190
LC ebook record available at https://lccn.loc.gov/2019056191

ISBN 978-1-9821-4108-0
ISBN 978-1-9821-4109-7 (ebook)

CONTENTS

THERE'S NO REAL SECRET TO COOKING IN FOIL.

As a casual variation on the French technique of *en papillote*, or *al cartoccio* in Italian, foil pack dinners present an even simpler way to steam-cook seasoned meat or vegetables. A pouch is created by folding aluminum foil and sealing the ends. When heated, the food cooks in a sauce or in its own juices. Contained in the packet, the moist heat locks in flavor and keeps food juicy. The finished dish can be eaten directly from the package or slid onto a plate or bowl.

ALUMINUM FOIL 101

HEAVY-DUTY FOIL

Sturdier than standard foil, heavy-duty aluminum foil is the most commonly used variety when creating packets. Available in twelve-inch and eighteen-inch widths, heavy-duty foil can cover any size bundle of food or cut of beef. Cheese and sugary foods will stick, so the interior should be coated with food spray, butter, or oil.

HEAVY-DUTY NONSTICK FOIL

Hands down the most convenient foil for all uses is nonstick. One side of the foil is coated in a silicone-based polymer that makes food slide right off. Note: All rolls of aluminum foil have shiny and dull sides due to how they're produced. In theory, the shiny side will reflect heat while the dull side absorbs it. Manufacturers say the difference is negligible and either side may be used; however, this is *not* the case for the nonstick foils. The food-safe, nonstick coating is on the dull side and will also be imprinted with the words "nonstick side."

GRILLING FOIL

This type of foil is designed to withstand the very high temperatures grills can reach, up to 600°F. Some versions have a nonstick coating for convenience. You may see "pitmasters" foil. This type is extra-thick and strong enough for large and heavy cuts.

RECYCLED FOIL

This foil is made from recycled aluminum that has been heated to high temperatures to ensure food safety. Aluminum foil can be recycled, but you will need to confirm that your local recycling station accepts it.

GRILLING BAGS

These foil bags are constructed so you only have to place the food inside and roll up one end. Some versions have clear plastic windows so you can see the food cooking. Place the bags on a rimmed baking sheet before opening and cut open from the top.

STANDARD FOIL

Avoid using standard foil for foil packs. If there's no way around it, use double or triple thickness. A single ply of regular foil is too thin. It can tear easily, resulting in a mess or a lost meal on the bottom of your oven or grill. Its thinness also means foods can scorch on the bottom.

TYPES OF PACKAGES

FLAT PACKAGES

Foods that benefit from browning, such as burgers and steaks, are often cooked in flat packages. Another reason to cover the meal in a flat package is when the recipe calls for flipping the package over to cook the other side. Use flat packs when the food can be turned with little risk of spilling liquid.

HOW TO ASSEMBLE

1. Place ingredient(s) in the center of the foil.

2. Bring the edges of the long sides of the foil together on top. Fold the foil several times until it is flat against the ingredients.

3. Fold up the sides several times until flush against the food.

4. To turn over while cooking, slide a silicone-coated or wooden spatula carefully under the package and flip over. Take care that the spatula does not pierce the foil. Plastic- or silicone-tipped tongs can also be used to turn the packages.

TENT-STYLE PACKAGES

Tent-style packages encourage steam produced by the cooking food to condense and drip back down over the food, basting it with moisture and flavor. They are assembled so that there's a pocket of air above the food.

HOW TO ASSEMBLE

1. Place the ingredients in the center of the foil.

2. Bring the edges of the long sides of the foil together on top. Fold a couple of times, leaving air space above the food.

3. Fold up the sides, folding several times until they're completely sealed.

4. If necessary, rotate the packages or move to hotter/cooler areas of your grill by gripping the top seal with tongs. Any tongs may be used, but silicone- or plastic-tipped ones are less likely to tear the foil.

FOIL PACKETS 101

GO LARGE—IT'S BETTER TO OVERESTIMATE THE SIZE YOU'LL NEED TO WRAP THE MEAL. If you aren't keen on measuring, make sure the foil sheet is twice as long as the area of the food. The foil is too small if you can't get at least two or three folds at the seams. If there's doubt, tear off a new piece. Alternatively, you can place the too-small foil package in a larger piece of foil and seal the outer one.

CHEESE AND SUGARY FOODS LIKE JAM OR HONEY MAY STICK TO THE FOIL. Use nonstick foil, spray the interior side of the foil with cooking spray, or line the foil package with parchment paper.

CUT DENSE AND LONG-COOKING FOODS INTO THIN SLICES OR SMALL CUBES so they finish cooking at the same time as the rest of the meal.

SEASON, SEASON, SEASON! Moisture doesn't evaporate and will dilute herbs and spices. Season your food liberally.

CHICKENS ARE GROWING BIGGER! A serving of boneless chicken ranges from four to six ounces, yet chicken breasts can often be nine or ten ounces. Larger breasts will take longer to cook, and the exterior of the meat can become tough. Vegetables cooked with larger pieces of chicken may become overcooked. To solve this, use chicken breast cutlets you can purchase in the meat section, or split a thick chicken breast in half lengthwise.

ARRANGE THE LONGEST-COOKING FOODS (LIKE POTATOES OR OTHER DENSE FOODS) ON THE BOTTOM OF THE PACKAGE. The bottom is likely to receive the most heat, and foods placed there will cook a little bit faster.

PLAN FOR TOO MUCH LIQUID. Vegetables hold a lot of water. As they cook, this moisture essentially steams the remaining ingredients. Occasionally too much water settles at the bottom of the pack. This highly seasoned liquid shouldn't be poured off! Placing cooked rice, quinoa, or other grains on the bottom soaks up the thin "gravy" and bulks up the serving.

FOLD, DON'T BUNCH. Fold the edges of the foil as neatly as possible. If you need to check the contents to see if the food is done, folded seams are easier to open and reseal, and will be less likely to tear.

WHILE MANY FOIL PACKAGES CAN BE MADE AHEAD, TRANSPORTING THEM IN A COOLER IS TRICKY. Edges of other packages and ice packs can tear the foil, allowing melted ice water to seep in.

IF TRANSPORTING, PACKAGES SHOULD NOT BE STACKED ON TOP OF ONE ANOTHER, ESPECIALLY TENT-STYLE PACKAGES. Ideally the portions are divided as the recipe directs, but if you need to apportion them ahead of time, you can divide the portions, place them in plastic storage bags, and chill them until you're ready to cook. Transfer the contents of each bag into a foil package made right before cooking.

WHEN GRILLING FOIL PACKETS, CHECK FOR HOT OR COOL SPOTS. Rotate the packages around the grill grates as necessary.

WHILE IT'S MUCH EASIER TO TRANSFER THE FOIL PACK TO A PLATE (ESPECIALLY IF CUTTING MEAT), eating directly from the foil means you won't have dishes to wash. Any leftovers can be folded over and refrigerated.

IN / ON / OVER

IN THE OVEN

Cooking foil packs in the oven is simple, since ovens offer the most consistent heat. If you have a convection oven, use that setting, as the fan will increase circulation around the foil packages, ensuring even cooking.

Preheat the oven to the required temperature, because cooking times are based on putting food into a hot oven. This is especially appropriate with foods containing leavening agents such as baking soda, baking powder, or yeast.

If tears or leaks occur when baking in the oven, transfer the packages to a rimmed baking sheet to continue cooking.

You can also tuck a large sheet of foil over the rack under the food. (Do not place foil on the bottom of the oven, as it will block heat and air flow.)

ON THE GRILL

Enjoy fine weather and keep your kitchen clean and cool by cooking your foil packages on a grill.

Propane and natural-gas grills are easy to get going. Assuming you have a full tank, the heat output will be consistent. Preheat the grill as you would an oven.

After lighting a charcoal grill, make sure the lumps or briquettes are covered with fine gray ash, a sign that they're hot.

Cover food. With either method, it's important to close the grill cover so the heat surrounds the food. By keeping the grill lid closed, the temperature remains steady and the packages are also heated from the top.

Cooking over direct heat is the most common way to grill. The food cooks directly over hot coals or gas grill outlets. You can change the intensity of the heat by raising or lowering the grill grate or opening the air vents. Most of the foil package recipes are cooked over direct heat. For quick-cooking foods, direct heat is ideal when the grill lid is closed.

Grilling over indirect heat is good for thick, bone-in meats and foods that require thirty minutes or more. To set up indirect heat, turn on all the burners, allowing the grill to preheat. Before adding the food, turn off the burners on one side and adjust the other burners according to how much heat is needed. You may need to increase or decrease the burners on the "hot side" to maintain consistent oven-like temperatures. Place the packages over the "cool side." If using charcoal, prepare the briquettes as you would a traditional grill, then carefully move the hot coals to one side.

OVER A CAMPFIRE

Primitive campers often cooked their food over a campfire. It's the most basic type of of alfresco cooking. While campfire cooking is authentic and somewhat romantic, the heat output is inconsistent. Rotate the packages with long-handled tongs to ensure even cooking. Check the wood or coals, adding more if necessary, to ensure that the fire remains low enough to cook food. If in doubt, prepare vegetarian meals or recipes with cooked meats (like smoked sausage or rotisserie chicken) to avoid eating undercooked meats that could pose a food-safety risk.

SAFETY TIPS

FOIL PACKAGES WILL BE VERY HOT WHEN REMOVED FROM THE OVEN OR THE GRILL. Use tongs and an oven mitt to remove the packages, and use the tongs and a fork to unfold the foil. If the packages are heavy, you can pinch the top with tongs and carefully slide a silicone or wooden spoon or spatula under the bottom to remove from the heat.

AS AN EXCELLENT CONDUCTOR OF HEAT, ALUMINUM FOIL GETS HOT—FAST! Even if the pack has been in the oven or on the grill for only two or three minutes, it may be too hot to touch. If you forget that sprinkle of cheese before you fold up the packages and want to add it before cooking any longer, remove the package with an oven mitt and tongs as though it's completely cooked.

SINCE FOIL COOKS THE FOODS WITHIN THE PACKET, THERE WILL BE PLENTY OF STEAM ESCAPING THE PACKAGES WHEN OPENED. Use a pair of tongs and a fork to unfold and separate the foil seams.

THERE MAY BE (BOILING) HOT LIQUID ALONG WITH THE COOKED FOOD INSIDE THE PACKETS. Take care not to tear the foil when removing from the heat to avoid scalds or unfortunate messes. An easy safeguard is to remove the packages from the grill or oven and place on a rimmed baking sheet. Any spills will be contained, and tasty juices can be poured back over the food.

TO AVOID FOOD-BORNE ILLNESSES, KEEP POTENTIALLY HAZARDOUS FOOD AT THE PROPER TEMPERATURE. That means uncooked meats, eggs, dairy products, cooked rice, cooked pasta, and cut fruit and vegetables must be stored below 40°F. Keep wrapped packages in the refrigerator if prepping ahead.

MANY FOIL PACK DINNERS CAN BE MADE A FEW HOURS AHEAD AND HEATED WHEN CONVENIENT. Avoid wrapping high-acid foods, such as those with a lot of citrus juice or tomato-based ingredients, since the acids could interact with the aluminum and create holes in the foil wrapping.

IF YOU PREFER, PLACE A PIECE OF PARCHMENT PAPER ON THE BOTTOM OF FOIL PACKAGES BEFORE TOPPING WITH THE RAW INGREDIENTS. Or, wrap the food in parchment paper, folding the edges to secure, and then wrap the parchment pouch in aluminum foil and seal as directed.

NEVER COOK FOIL PACKAGES (OR USE ANY METAL) IN THE MICROWAVE. Microwaves pass through paper and glass, but they get deflected by foil. In a microwave, foil pouches won't cook evenly and can cause damage to the microwave oven.

CHAPTER 1

YARDBIRDS

Wrapping chicken in foil seals in its natural juices. Season it well and add a handful of fresh vegetables, and your meal will be moist and delicious.

Ubiquitous chicken breasts are versatile and make an ideal base for a wide variety of herbs and spices.

Mild and inexpensive, chicken is the most invited meat to the dinner table. One reason chicken is the most sought-after protein is also its greatest flaw—blandness. While the birds don't necessarily fly, their popularity is soaring. As a result, the most requested parts, like breasts, are coming to market heavier than ever. While you may consider one boneless chicken breast to be one serving, you could be far off the mark. The average portion size for chicken ranges from four ounces in a low-fat cookbook to up to six ounces for a typical serving. Open a package from the market, however, and a single breast can weigh up to ten ounces. This is problematic for foil packet dinners and all other methods of cooking: it takes longer than anticipated to reach the proper interior temperature, while the exterior overcooks and becomes tough. To solve this, slice one oversized chicken breast in half lengthwise to create two cutlets.

Consider substituting chicken thighs for breasts. Their darker meat has more flavor and moisture, since it has more fat than breasts. Thighs come in manageable sizes, sometimes on the small side. One may be too skimpy a serving, so double up to get a good six-ounce portion.

RECIPE LIST

×

BARBECUE CHICKEN SWEET POTATO BOATS

2 large sweet potatoes or russet potatoes, cooked

1 tablespoon melted butter or olive oil

¼ teaspoon fine sea salt

⅛ teaspoon freshly ground black pepper

2 cups shredded grilled or rotisserie chicken

⅓ cup Molasses BBQ Sauce (page 53) or purchased barbecue sauce

4 slices provolone, mozzarella, or cheddar cheese

3 green onions, sliced

Sweet potatoes are a rich source of beta carotene and fiber. Aside from their health benefits, sweet potatoes are a delicious vegetable. They need to be cooked for this recipe. Bake for 35 to 40 minutes at 350°F or microwave on high for 5 to 8 minutes until the center is tender when pierced with a knife.

OVEN TEMPERATURE 350°F   **GRILL** MEDIUM HEAT
FOIL 4 SHEETS NONSTICK FOIL OR FOIL LIGHTLY COATED WITH COOKING SPRAY
SIZE 12" X 12"   **TENT-STYLE** PACKAGE   **SERVES** 4

---

1 Preheat the oven to 350°F or your grill to medium heat.

2 Slice each potato in half lengthwise. Scoop out the insides into a medium bowl, leaving a ¼-inch shell. Brush the inside of the potato shells with the melted butter or oil. Sprinkle the inside of the potatoes evenly with salt and pepper. Bake for about 10 minutes, until the shells are dry and starting to brown on the edges. (Note: this step is optional, but it makes the shells sturdier for holding the filling as well as adding more flavor and texture.)

3 Add the chicken and barbecue sauce to the bowl with the potato. Stir until well blended. Spoon the chicken mixture evenly into the potato shells. Place a slice of cheese over each potato. Sprinkle the top evenly with green onions. Place in the center of each piece of foil.

4 Fold the foil over the mixture and crimp the edges for tent-style packages. For convenience, you can also cook two potato boats, side by side, in one piece of foil. Cook for 25 minutes, until the potato boats are hot and the cheese is melted.

BOURSIN-BASIL STUFFED CHICKEN

4 (4-ounce) chicken cutlets

1 (5.2-ounce) package
   Boursin cheese

¼ cup very loosely packed
   fresh basil leaves

4 thin slices prosciutto

1½ cups cooked pasta
   or rice

You can find Boursin cheese in the deli section of markets in a variety of flavors—use your favorite. Goat cheese lovers can substitute their favorite as well. If you prefer something very mild, use plain cream cheese and add a bit of salt and pepper for seasoning.

✕

OVEN TEMPERATURE 350°F   **GRILL** MEDIUM HEAT
FOIL 2 SHEETS NONSTICK FOIL OR
FOIL LIGHTLY COATED WITH COOKING SPRAY
SIZE 12" X 15"   **TENT-STYLE** PACKAGE   **SERVES** 2

✕

1 Preheat the oven to 350°F or your grill to medium heat.

2 Place the chicken cutlets flat on a cutting board. Spread 2 tablespoons of the Boursin cheese evenly on the top side. Divide the basil leaves and press onto the cheese.

3 Roll each cutlet into a spiral and wrap with a slice of prosciutto. Spoon the pasta evenly into the center of each piece of foil. Top with 2 spirals.

4 Fold the foil over the chicken and crimp the edges for tent-style packages. Cook for 25 minutes, until the chicken is cooked through.

CHICKEN AND DUMPLINGS

The dumplings in this homey comfort dish cook by the heat of the oven and the steam from the chicken mixture. They will need room to expand, so make sure there's air space on top when you seal the package.

3 cups shredded rotisserie or cooked chicken

2 carrots, shredded

½ cup chopped slender green beans or baby peas

⅓ cup chopped onion

2 tablespoons butter, melted

4 ounces cream cheese

½ teaspoon poultry seasoning

1 teaspoon fine sea salt

¼ teaspoon freshly ground black pepper

1 cup self-rising flour

2 tablespoons cold butter, cut into pieces

½ cup milk, chicken broth, or water

OVEN TEMPERATURE 350°F   **GRILL** MEDIUM HEAT
FOIL 4 SHEETS NONSTICK FOIL OR FOIL LIGHTLY COATED WITH COOKING SPRAY
SIZE 12" X 24"   **TENT-STYLE** PACKAGE   **SERVES** 4

---

1 Preheat the oven to 350°F or your grill to medium heat.

2 Combine the chicken, carrots, beans or peas, and onion in a large bowl, stirring until well blended.

3 Mix the melted butter and cream cheese in a small bowl. Cook in the microwave on medium power for 30 to 60 seconds, until melted. Stir in the poultry seasoning, salt, and pepper. Stir the butter mixture into the chicken mixture.

4 Spoon the chicken mixture evenly into the center of each piece of foil.

5 Add the flour to the large bowl (no need to wash). Cut in the butter with a pastry blender or fork until the mixture is crumbly. Add the milk, chicken broth, or water, stirring until the dough comes together. Dollop the dough by tablespoons evenly over the chicken mixture.

6 Fold the foil over the mixture and crimp the edges for tent-style packages. Cook for 30 minutes, until the mixture is hot and the dumplings are cooked.

CREAMY CHICKEN AND GREEN CHILE ENCHILADAS

Corn tortillas are tender and can tear or crumble with the weight of the filling ingredients, especially if cold. Warm the tortillas in the oven for a few minutes to make them more pliable. Be sure not to overcook, as they will begin to crisp into tostadas if heated too long.

✕

OVEN TEMPERATURE 350°F **GRILL** MEDIUM HEAT
FOIL 5 SHEETS NONSTICK FOIL OR
FOIL LIGHTLY COATED WITH COOKING SPRAY
SIZE 12" X 18" **TENT-STYLE** PACKAGE (ENCHILADAS)
FLAT PACKAGE (TORTILLAS) **SERVES** 4

✕

1 tablespoon olive oil

1 small onion, chopped

2 small garlic cloves, minced

12 (5-inch) corn tortillas, warmed

4 ounces cream cheese, softened

¼ cup sour cream

1 (4-ounce) can diced green chilies, drained

3 cups shredded rotisserie chicken

½ teaspoon fine sea salt

¼ teaspoon freshly ground black pepper

1 cup Quick Enchilada Sauce (recipe opposite) or green tomatillo salsa

1 cup (4 ounces) shredded cheddar cheese

1 Preheat the oven to 350°F or your grill to medium heat.

2 Heat the oil in a large nonstick skillet over medium-high heat. Add the onion and garlic; cook, stirring frequently, for 5 to 8 minutes until the onions are tender.

3 Meanwhile, wrap the tortillas in a piece of foil and crimp the edges for a flat package. Cook for 5 minutes, until warm and pliable. Leave the tortillas in the foil until ready to assemble.

4 Reduce the skillet heat to medium. Add the cream cheese, sour cream, and chilies. Cook, stirring frequently, until the cheese melts and the mixture is evenly blended. Stir in the chicken, salt, and pepper.

5 Spoon 2 tablespoons of the enchilada sauce or salsa into the center of each piece of foil. Fill each tortilla with ¼ cup of the chicken mixture. Roll and place the enchiladas, seam side down, on the sauce. Drizzle with an additional 2 tablespoons sauce. Sprinkle with 1 heaping tablespoon of cheese.

6 Fold the foil over the mixture and crimp the edges for tent-style packages. Cook for 25 minutes, until the mixture is hot and the cheese is melted.

QUICK ENCHILADA SAUCE

1 cup vegetable broth

1 tablespoon extra-virgin olive oil

1 tablespoon all-purpose flour

1 tablespoon chili powder

1 tablespoon tomato paste

1 tablespoon apple cider vinegar

2 teaspoons ground cumin

1 teaspoon chipotle peppers in adobo sauce, minced (optional)

¼ teaspoon garlic powder

¼ teaspoon salt

Whisk together all of the ingredients in a small saucepan over medium-low heat. Simmer for 5 minutes, stirring occasionally, until the mixture thickens. MAKES 1 CUP

CHICKEN AND SHRIMP PAELLA

Saffron is the distinguishing flavor of paella and is considered the world's most expensive spice. Luckily, it doesn't take much to add a lot of flavor. Saffron threads hold flavor longer than powdered saffron. Crumble the pieces between your fingers just before using.

1 (15.5-ounce) can fire-roasted diced tomatoes, drained

¼ cup white wine

2 tablespoons extra-virgin olive oil

1 teaspoon fine sea salt

1 teaspoon paprika or smoked paprika

½ teaspoon saffron, crumbled

4 boneless, skinless chicken thighs, cut into pieces

½ pound peeled and deveined uncooked shrimp

4 ounces smoked sausage, sliced

½ onion, thinly sliced

3 cups cooked medium- or long-grain rice

1 (6.5-ounce) can chopped clams, drained and rinsed (optional)

2 tablespoons chopped fresh flat-leaf parsley

OVEN TEMPERATURE 375°F **GRILL** MEDIUM HEAT
FOIL 4 SHEETS NONSTICK FOIL OR FOIL LIGHTLY COATED WITH COOKING SPRAY
SIZE 18" X 24" **TENT-STYLE** PACKAGE **SERVES** 4

1 Preheat the oven to 375°F or your grill to medium heat.

2 Combine the tomatoes, wine, oil, salt, paprika, and saffron in a large bowl. Add the chicken, shrimp, sausage, and onion, tossing to coat. Add the rice, stirring until well blended.

3 Spoon the chicken mixture evenly into the center of each piece of foil. Top evenly with the clams, if desired.

4 Fold the foil over the mixture and crimp the edges for tent-style packages. Cook for 30 minutes, until the mixture is hot and the chicken and shrimp are cooked through. Open the foil and sprinkle each serving evenly with chopped parsley.

CHICKEN CORDON BLEU

3 tablespoons
   mayonnaise

1 tablespoon Dijon
   mustard

½ teaspoon fine sea salt

¼ teaspoon freshly
   ground black pepper

½ cup seasoned panko
   breadcrumbs

2 cups cooked rice

4 (6-ounce) chicken
   breasts

4 slices ham

4 slices Swiss cheese

To make this easy dish keto-friendly, swap the breadcrumbs for shredded Parmesan cheese and riced cauliflower for the rice. Both versions are equally delicious.

OVEN TEMPERATURE 350°F   **GRILL** MEDIUM HEAT
FOIL 4 SHEETS NONSTICK FOIL OR
FOIL LIGHTLY COATED WITH COOKING SPRAY
SIZE 12" X 15"   **TENT-STYLE** PACKAGE   **SERVES** 4

---

1 Preheat the oven to 350°F or your grill to medium heat.

2 Combine the mayonnaise, mustard, salt, and pepper in a small bowl. Place the breadcrumbs in a medium bowl. Spoon ½ cup of rice into the center of each piece of foil.

3 Place the chicken between two pieces of clear plastic wrap and pound to an even thickness. Brush the mayonnaise mixture over both sides. Dredge the chicken in the breadcrumbs and place on top of the rice. Top each chicken breast with one slice of ham and one slice of cheese.

4 Fold the foil over the mixture and crimp the edges for tent-style packages. Cook for 30 minutes, until the chicken is cooked through.

CHICKEN PICCATA

2 (6-ounce) chicken breasts or 1 (8- to 10-ounce) chicken breast

1 tablespoon all-purpose flour

2 tablespoons butter, melted

1 tablespoon white wine

1 teaspoon lemon zest

1 tablespoon fresh lemon juice

½ teaspoon chicken bouillon granules

2 teaspoons capers, rinsed and drained

2 tablespoons chopped fresh parsley

The small amount of flour dusted on the chicken thickens the juices that melt around it as it cooks. Adding broth would dilute the flavor too much, so a sprinkling of salty bouillon granules will add flavor without thinning the sauce.

✕

OVEN TEMPERATURE 375°F   **GRILL** MEDIUM HEAT
FOIL 4 SHEETS HEAVY-DUTY NONSTICK FOIL OR FOIL LIGHTLY COATED WITH COOKING SPRAY
SIZE 12" X 15"   **TENT-STYLE** PACKAGE   **SERVES** 2

✕
---

1 Preheat the oven to 375°F or your grill to medium heat.

2 If using one large chicken breast, slice it in half lengthwise, creating two cutlets. Place the chicken between two pieces of clear plastic wrap and pound to an even thickness. Dust the outside of the breast evenly with the flour and place in the center of each piece of foil.

3 Combine the butter, wine, lemon zest, lemon juice, bouillon granules, and capers in a small bowl. Drizzle evenly over the chicken. Sprinkle evenly with the parsley.

4 Fold the foil over the chicken and crimp the edges for tent-style packages. Cook for 35 minutes, until the chicken is cooked through.

CHICKEN WITH QUINOA PILAF

6 small or 4 large boneless, skinless chicken thighs, cut into pieces

3 cups cooked quinoa

1 cup lightly packed spinach or arugula

⅓ cup chopped toasted walnuts

¼ cup cherry tomatoes, halved, or sun-dried tomatoes

4 slices cooked bacon, chopped

¼ cup crumbled feta cheese

¼ cup olive oil

1 shallot, minced

¾ teaspoon fine sea salt

¼ teaspoon freshly ground black pepper

Nutty-tasting quinoa is an ancient seed crop that's used like a grain. Unlike other grains, it's considered a complete protein. Before cooking, rinse the quinoa in cold water. Toss a bouillon cube into the cooking water for extra flavor.

— × —

OVEN TEMPERATURE 375°F   **GRILL** MEDIUM HEAT
FOIL 4 SHEETS NONSTICK FOIL OR FOIL LIGHTLY COATED WITH COOKING SPRAY
SIZE 12" X 18"   **TENT-STYLE** PACKAGE   **SERVES** 4

— × —

1 Preheat the oven to 375°F or your grill to medium heat.

2 Combine the chicken, quinoa, spinach, walnuts, tomatoes, bacon, feta, oil, shallot, salt, and pepper in a large bowl.

3 Spoon the chicken mixture evenly into the center of each piece of foil.

4 Fold the foil over the mixture and crimp the edges for tent-style packages. Cook for 30 minutes, until the chicken is cooked through.

CHICKEN TERIYAKI MEATBALLS

Chicken or turkey meatballs make a lean dinner or snack option, but the meat is often very bland. Not in this recipe! Fresh ginger and sesame oil add bold flavor, especially when topped with the sweet-and-salty Teriyaki Glaze.

OVEN TEMPERATURE 375°F **GRILL** MEDIUM HEAT

FOIL 4 SHEETS NONSTICK FOIL OR FOIL LIGHTLY COATED WITH COOKING SPRAY

SIZE 12" X 18"   **TENT-STYLE** PACKAGE   **SERVES** 4

TERIYAKI GLAZE

½ cup firmly packed light brown sugar

½ cup soy sauce

1 tablespoon rice vinegar

1 teaspoon cornstarch

1¼ pounds ground chicken or turkey

¼ cup thinly sliced green onion

1½ tablespoons minced fresh ginger

¼ teaspoon garlic powder

½ teaspoon fine sea salt

1 teaspoon sesame oil

⅓ cup panko breadcrumbs

1 Preheat the oven to 375°F or your grill to medium heat.

2 Prepare the Teriyaki Glaze: Stir together the brown sugar, soy sauce, rice vinegar, and cornstarch in a small saucepan until well blended. Bring the sauce to a boil over medium-high heat; boil for 1 minute. Set aside.

3 Combine the chicken, onion, ginger, garlic powder, salt, oil, and breadcrumbs in a bowl, stirring with your hands until well blended. Roll the mixture into 1½-inch meatballs (about 20).

4 Divide the meatballs evenly in the center of the foil sheets. Drizzle the Teriyaki Glaze evenly over the meatballs, rolling them around to lightly coat.

5 Fold the foil over the mixture and crimp the edges for tent-style packages. Cook for 25 minutes, until the meatballs are cooked through.

CHICKEN WITH CREAMY TOMATO-BASIL SAUCE

4 ounces cream cheese

½ cup julienned Italian-seasoned sun-dried tomatoes

¼ cup shredded or grated Parmesan cheese

¼ cup fresh basil leaves, minced

1 tablespoon white wine

½ teaspoon fine sea salt

¼ teaspoon freshly ground black pepper

12 ounces boneless, skinless chicken breasts or cutlets

4 ounces cremini or button mushrooms, sliced

Cremini mushrooms are the "baby" form of portobellos. These dark brown mushrooms have an earthier flavor, but you can substitute any mushroom you desire. Dry- or oil-packed dried tomatoes can be used as long as the dried ones are still soft and tender.

OVEN TEMPERATURE 350°F   **GRILL** MEDIUM HEAT
FOIL 4 SHEETS NONSTICK FOIL OR FOIL LIGHTLY COATED WITH COOKING SPRAY
SIZE 12" X 15"   **TENT-STYLE** PACKAGE   **SERVES** 2

---

1 Preheat the oven to 350°F or your grill to medium heat.

2 Place the cream cheese in a glass bowl and microwave on high for 30 seconds, until the cheese is very soft and almost melted. Stir in the tomatoes, Parmesan, basil, wine, salt, and pepper. Set aside.

3 Place the chicken breasts on a cutting board. Hold each breast flat with one hand and, using a sharp knife in your other hand, slice the chicken breast horizontally into two even pieces. Place each cutlet between two sheets of plastic wrap and pound to an even thickness.

4 Divide the chicken evenly and place in the center of each piece of foil. Divide the mushrooms evenly and place over the chicken. Dollop the cheese mixture on top.

5 Fold the foil over the mixture and crimp the edges for tent-style packages. Cook for 40 minutes, until the chicken is cooked through.

CHICKEN WITH ROOT VEGGIES

3 tablespoons butter, melted

2 garlic cloves, minced

2 teaspoons chopped fresh rosemary

1 teaspoon fine sea salt

1 teaspoon freshly ground black pepper

1 cup baby carrots, halved lengthwise

1 sweet onion, cut into thin wedges

3 small red or yellow beets, peeled and chopped

8 radishes, halved

1 lemon, thinly sliced

1¼ pounds boneless, skinless chicken thighs, cutlets, or breasts

Beets are polarizing. Aside from their health benefits, diners either love or hate them. If you relate to the latter, simply substitute russet or sweet potatoes. Beet lovers won't be alarmed when the dish takes on a pinkish hue when cooked, as they're used to the vibrant color that spreads around the dish.

✕

OVEN TEMPERATURE 375°F   **GRILL** MEDIUM HEAT

FOIL 4 SHEETS HEAVY-DUTY NONSTICK FOIL OR FOIL LIGHTLY COATED WITH COOKING SPRAY

SIZE 12" X 18"   **TENT-STYLE** PACKAGE   **SERVES** 4

✕
---

1 Preheat the oven to 375°F or your grill to medium heat.

2 Combine the butter, garlic, rosemary, salt, and pepper in a large bowl. Stir in the carrots, onion, beets, radishes, and lemon. Place the vegetables in the center of each piece of foil.

3 If using chicken breasts, slice each one in half lengthwise to form cutlets. Place between sheets of plastic wrap and pound to an even thickness. Arrange the chicken evenly over the vegetables. Drizzle any seasoned butter left in the bowl over the chicken.

4 Fold the foil over the vegetables and crimp the edges for tent-style packages. Cook for 50 minutes, until the chicken is cooked through and the vegetables are tender.

CHIPOTLE-ORANGE CHICKEN

½ cup orange marmalade

1 tablespoon white balsamic or white wine vinegar

1 teaspoon chipotle peppers in adobo sauce, minced

1 teaspoon fine sea salt

½ teaspoon ground cumin

½ teaspoon freshly ground black pepper

4 boneless, skinless chicken thighs

2 cups cooked rice

2 teaspoons chopped fresh cilantro

The spicy, smoked jalapeños, called chipotle chilies, are commonly sold immersed in adobo sauce in cans. The seeds are particularly hot, and you can omit them if you want a milder dish. Remember to wash your hands after touching the peppers.

OVEN TEMPERATURE 350°F   **GRILL** MEDIUM HEAT
FOIL 4 SHEETS NONSTICK FOIL OR
FOIL LIGHTLY COATED WITH COOKING SPRAY
SIZE 12" X 15"   **TENT-STYLE** PACKAGE   **SERVES** 4

---

1 Preheat the oven to 350°F or your grill to medium heat.

2 Combine the orange marmalade, vinegar, chipotle peppers, salt, cumin, and pepper in a large bowl. Add the chicken, tossing to coat.

3 Combine the rice and cilantro, stirring until well blended. Spoon ½ cup of the rice into the center of each piece of foil. Divide the chicken evenly and place over the rice. Drizzle the liquid from the bowl evenly over the chicken.

4 Fold the foil over the chicken and crimp the edges for tent-style packages. Cook for 35 minutes, until the chicken is cooked through.

GREEK CHICKEN WITH OLIVES AND FETA

2 tomatoes, seeded and chopped

½ red onion, thinly sliced

¼ cup pitted Kalamata olives, halved

2 garlic cloves, minced

3 tablespoons chopped fresh flat-leaf parsley

1 tablespoon chopped fresh oregano

1 teaspoon lemon zest

1 tablespoon fresh lemon juice

¼ teaspoon freshly ground black pepper

½ cup (4 ounces) crumbled feta cheese

4 (4- to 6-ounce) chicken breasts

2 cups cooked orzo or rice

Many packaged chicken breasts are enormous—up to 10 ounces each—but organic and free-range versions are closer to a healthy portion size. If the breasts are thicker than 1 inch, slice them in half horizontally rather than trying to pound them to an even thickness.

OVEN TEMPERATURE 375°F **GRILL** MEDIUM HEAT
FOIL 4 SHEETS NONSTICK FOIL OR FOIL LIGHTLY COATED WITH COOKING SPRAY
SIZE 12" X 15" **TENT-STYLE** PACKAGE **SERVES** 4

---

1 Preheat the oven to 375°F or your grill to medium heat.

2 Combine the tomatoes, onion, olives, garlic, parsley, oregano, lemon zest, lemon juice, pepper, and feta in a medium bowl.

3 Place the chicken between two pieces of clear plastic wrap and pound to an even thickness. Spoon ½ cup of the orzo into the center of each piece of foil. Top the orzo with a chicken breast. Top the chicken evenly with the tomato mixture.

4 Seal and crimp the edges for tent-style packages. Cook for 30 minutes, until the chicken is cooked through.

CILANTRO-PEPITA PESTO WITH CHICKEN AND RICE

1 bunch fresh cilantro

1 teaspoon lime zest

2 tablespoons fresh lime juice

1 garlic clove, coarsely chopped

1 teaspoon fine sea salt

1 teaspoon ground cumin

Pinch of crushed red pepper flakes

3 tablespoons extra-virgin olive oil

2 tablespoons toasted pumpkin seeds (pepitas)

2 cups cooked rice

4 (6-ounce) boneless, skinless chicken thighs or breasts

Use a food processor with a small bowl, if possible, since this is a small batch. If you prefer, you can finely chop all the ingredients. If using large breasts, cut them in half lengthwise to create cutlets.

OVEN TEMPERATURE 350°F   **GRILL** MEDIUM HEAT
FOIL 4 SHEETS NONSTICK FOIL OR
FOIL LIGHTLY COATED WITH COOKING SPRAY
SIZE 12" X 15"   **TENT-STYLE** PACKAGE   **SERVES** 4

---

1 Preheat the oven to 350°F or your grill to medium heat.

2 Combine the cilantro, lime zest, lime juice, garlic, salt, cumin, pepper flakes, and oil in a food processor. Process until the mixture is somewhat smooth, scraping down the sides of the processor with a spatula if necessary. Add the pumpkin seeds; process until the seeds are finely chopped.

3 Spoon ½ cup of the rice into the center of each piece of foil. Top with a chicken thigh. Top the chicken evenly with the pesto mixture.

4 Seal and crimp the edges for tent-style packages. Cook for 30 minutes, until the chicken is cooked through.

HOT CHICKEN, BACON, AND CORN SALAD

This delicious and versatile recipe can be enjoyed many ways—use whatever citrus you have and substitute your favorite bean or vegetable, such as chopped zucchini, for the corn.

OVEN TEMPERATURE 350°F   **GRILL** MEDIUM HEAT
FOIL 2 SHEETS NONSTICK FOIL OR
FOIL LIGHTLY COATED WITH COOKING SPRAY
SIZE 12" X 18"   **TENT-STYLE** PACKAGE   **SERVES** 4

---

2 tablespoons extra-virgin olive oil

1 teaspoon lime or lemon zest

2 tablespoons fresh lime or lemon juice

1 tablespoon honey

2 teaspoons Dijon mustard

1 garlic clove, minced

¾ teaspoon fine sea salt

¼ teaspoon freshly ground black pepper

3 cups shredded or chopped rotisserie chicken

2 cups fresh, frozen, or canned corn kernels

4 slices thick-cut bacon, cooked and chopped

½ cup shredded Parmesan cheese (optional)

¼ red onion, thinly sliced

3 cups baby arugula or spinach (optional)

1 avocado, cubed (optional)

2 tablespoons chopped fresh basil (optional)

1 Preheat the oven to 350°F or your grill to medium heat.

2 Combine the oil, lime zest, lime juice, honey, mustard, garlic, salt, and pepper in a large bowl.

3 Stir in the chicken, corn, bacon, Parmesan (if using), and onion. Divide the mixture evenly on each piece of foil.

4 Fold the foil over the chicken mixture and crimp the edges for tent-style packages. Cook for 25 minutes, until thoroughly hot. Serve as is, or serve the chicken mixture over fresh arugula topped with avocado and basil.

HONEY CHICKEN WITH COWBOY CAVIAR

2 tablespoons olive oil

1 teaspoon lime zest

2 tablespoons fresh lime juice

1 tablespoon ground cumin

1 teaspoon fine sea salt

½ teaspoon freshly ground black pepper

1 tablespoon honey

1½ pounds boneless, skinless chicken thighs or breasts

1 (15.5-ounce) can black-eyed peas, rinsed and drained

½ cup fresh or frozen corn kernels, thawed

1 large ripe tomato, quartered and seeded

¼ small red onion, chopped

1 garlic clove, minced

2 tablespoons chopped fresh cilantro

1 small avocado, cubed

If you want to serve the black-eyed pea salsa chilled or on the side, simply cook the seasoned chicken by itself. Cooking time will be shortened to 10 minutes. You can also swap black beans for the black-eyed peas.

×

OVEN TEMPERATURE 375°F   **GRILL** MEDIUM HEAT
FOIL 4 SHEETS NONSTICK FOIL OR
FOIL LIGHTLY COATED WITH COOKING SPRAY
SIZE 12" X 18"   **TENT-STYLE** PACKAGE   **SERVES** 4

×

---

1 Preheat the oven to 375°F or your grill to medium heat.

2 Combine 1 tablespoon oil, ½ teaspoon lime zest, 1 tablespoon lime juice, 1 teaspoon cumin, ½ teaspoon salt, the pepper, and honey in a medium bowl.

3 Divide the chicken evenly into four portions. If using large breasts, slice them in half lengthwise to create cutlets. Stir the chicken into the oil mixture, tossing until coated. Set aside.

4 Combine the black-eyed peas, corn, tomato, onion, garlic, cilantro, remaining 2 teaspoons cumin, remaining ½ teaspoon salt, remaining ½ teaspoon lime zest, and remaining 1 tablespoon lime juice in a large bowl.

5 Place the chicken evenly in the center of each piece of foil. Divide the black-eyed pea mixture and top the chicken evenly.

6 Fold the foil over the chicken mixture and crimp the edges for tent-style packages. Cook for 30 minutes, until the chicken is cooked through. Serve topped with avocado.

STICKY CHILEAN CHICKEN THIGHS WITH BROCCOLI AND RICE

½ cup sugar

2 teaspoons ancho chili powder

1 teaspoon ground cumin

¼ teaspoon red chili flakes

1 cup water

½ cup white wine vinegar

½ cup soy sauce

1½ cups cooked white or brown rice

3 cups broccoli florets

1½ pounds boneless, skinless chicken thighs, trimmed

¼ cup chopped fresh cilantro

This spicy-tangy sauce is a perfect match for hearty chicken thighs. The first step takes a few minutes, but it's important to reduce the sauce before assembling since it will dilute as the broccoli and chicken steam-cooks.

—————————— ✕ ——————————

OVEN TEMPERATURE 350°F   **GRILL** MEDIUM HEAT
FOIL 4 SHEETS NONSTICK FOIL OR
FOIL LIGHTLY COATED WITH COOKING SPRAY
SIZE 12" X 18"   **TENT-STYLE** PACKAGE   **SERVES** 4

—————————— ✕ ——————————

1 Combine the sugar, chili powder, cumin, chili flakes, water, vinegar, and soy sauce in a small saucepan. Bring to a boil over medium-high heat. Reduce the heat to medium and simmer, uncovered, for 20 minutes, until the mixture is thickened. Set aside.

2 Preheat the oven to 350°F or your grill to medium heat.

3 Divide the rice and broccoli evenly in the center of each piece of foil. Top the vegetables evenly with the chicken thighs. Brush the sauce evenly over the chicken.

4 Fold the foil over the mixture and crimp the edges for tent-style packages. Cook for 30 minutes, until the chicken is cooked through. Sprinkle with cilantro before serving.

HUNTER'S CHICKEN AND RICE

1 (15.5-ounce) can fire-roasted diced tomatoes, drained

2 tablespoons tomato paste

1 tablespoon cognac or white wine

2 tablespoons melted butter

1 tablespoon chopped fresh parsley

1 teaspoon fresh or dried tarragon

¾ teaspoon fine sea salt

1 (8-ounce) package cremini or button mushrooms, sliced

2 shallots, minced

1½ pounds boneless, skinless chicken thighs, cut into pieces

2 cups cooked rice

Chicken thighs are a fantastic choice for this hearty stew-like dish. Thighs are very tender and are considered more flavorful than breasts.

✗

OVEN TEMPERATURE 375°F   **GRILL** MEDIUM HEAT
FOIL 4 SHEETS NONSTICK FOIL OR FOIL LIGHTLY COATED WITH COOKING SPRAY
SIZE 12" X 18"   **TENT-STYLE** PACKAGE   **SERVES** 4

✗

1 Preheat the oven to 375°F or your grill to medium heat.

2 Combine the tomatoes, tomato paste, cognac, butter, parsley, tarragon, and salt in a large bowl. Stir in the mushrooms, shallots, and chicken.

3 Spoon ½ cup of the rice onto each piece of foil. Top the rice evenly with the chicken mixture.

4 Fold the foil over the mixture and crimp the edges for tent-style packages. Cook for 35 minutes, until the mixture is hot and the chicken is cooked through.

QUICK MARINATED CHICKEN AND SUMMER VEGETABLES

¼ cup fresh lemon juice

2 tablespoons extra-virgin olive oil

1 large garlic clove, minced

1 teaspoon light brown sugar

1 teaspoon chili powder

½ teaspoon ground cumin

½ teaspoon fine sea salt

¼ teaspoon crushed red pepper flakes

4 (6-ounce) boneless, skinless chicken breasts or 8 boneless, skinless chicken thighs

3 zucchini or yellow squash, halved and sliced

For even more flavor, you can marinate the chicken for an hour or two in a glass baking dish, a shallow bowl, or a plastic storage bag before assembling in the foil package. If you like, substitute a pound of fresh asparagus that's been trimmed and placed in a single layer under the chicken for the squash.

OVEN TEMPERATURE 350°F   **GRILL** MEDIUM HEAT
FOIL 4 SHEETS NONSTICK FOIL OR FOIL LIGHTLY COATED WITH COOKING SPRAY
SIZE 12" X 18"   **TENT-STYLE** PACKAGE   **SERVES** 4

---

1 Combine the lemon juice, oil, garlic, brown sugar, chili powder, cumin, salt, and pepper flakes in a small bowl.

2 Place the chicken between two sheets of plastic wrap and pound to an even thickness. Brush the chicken with the marinade; cover and chill for at least 15 minutes.

3 Preheat the oven to 350°F or your grill to medium heat.

4 Divide the squash evenly among the foil pieces. Top each evenly with the chicken, drizzling any liquid over the top.

5 Fold the foil over the mixture and crimp the edges for tent-style packages. Cook for 25 minutes, until hot and the chicken is cooked through.

MOROCCAN CHICKEN WITH CHICKPEAS AND CARROTS

1 (15.5-ounce) can chickpeas, rinsed and drained

1 cup cherry tomatoes, halved

2 carrots, peeled and sliced

½ onion, thinly sliced

1¼ to 1½ pounds boneless, skinless chicken breasts, cut into strips

¼ cup chopped dried pitted dates or apricots

1½ teaspoons extra-virgin olive oil

¾ teaspoon lemon zest

1 tablespoon fresh lemon juice

4 teaspoons *ras el hanout* or Moroccan seasoning blend (recipe opposite)

1 teaspoon fine sea salt

½ teaspoon freshly ground black pepper

Ras el hanout is an elaborate spice blend that can contain up to fifty different spices and herbs. You can substitute a prepared Moroccan seasoning blend or make the very simple version in the recipe opposite.

×

OVEN TEMPERATURE 375°F   **GRILL** MEDIUM HEAT
FOIL 4 SHEETS NONSTICK FOIL OR FOIL LIGHTLY COATED WITH COOKING SPRAY
SIZE 12" X 18"   **TENT-STYLE** PACKAGE   **SERVES** 4

×

1 Preheat the oven to 375°F or your grill to medium heat.

2 Combine the chickpeas, tomatoes, carrots, onion, chicken, and dates in a large bowl. Stir in the oil, lemon zest, lemon juice, seasoning blend, salt, and pepper. Divide the mixture evenly on the foil sheets.

3 Fold the foil over the mixture and crimp the edges for tent-style packages. Cook for 30 minutes, until hot and the chicken is cooked through.

MOROCCAN SEASONING BLEND

1½ teaspoons smoked
   paprika

1½ teaspoons ground cumin

1 teaspoon ground coriander

⅛ teaspoon ground
   cinnamon

Combine all the ingredients in a small bowl.

THAI CHICKEN CURRY WITH CAULIFLOWER RICE

2 tablespoons unsweetened cream of coconut (see Note)

2 teaspoons light brown sugar

1 tablespoon red curry or Penang curry paste

1 teaspoon fish sauce or soy sauce

1 teaspoon lime zest

2 tablespoons fresh lime juice

2 tablespoons chopped fresh basil

½ to ¾ pound boneless, skinless chicken breasts

1 red bell pepper, thinly sliced

½ onion, thinly sliced

1½ cups riced cauliflower

NOTE Unsweetened coconut cream isn't as easy to locate in markets as coconut milk. Cream of coconut, found near the cocktail-making ingredients, is too sweet. If you can't find it, purchase regular coconut milk (not the light variety) and use the thick portion that usually floats at the top of the can.

"Riced" cauliflower as a substitute for long-grain rice became trendy with the popularity of keto and low-carb diets. If you purchase frozen riced cauliflower, make sure it's completely thawed and well drained so the packages don't get too waterlogged. If using fresh cauliflower, remove the core from the cauliflower and cut into small florets. Place in a food processor and pulse several times, scraping down the sides with a spatula, until the cauliflower resembles rice.

OVEN TEMPERATURE 350°F **GRILL** MEDIUM HEAT
FOIL 4 SHEETS NONSTICK FOIL OR FOIL LIGHTLY COATED WITH COOKING SPRAY
SIZE 12" X 18" **TENT-STYLE** PACKAGE **SERVES** 4

---

1 Preheat the oven to 350°F or your grill to medium heat.

2 Combine the cream of coconut, brown sugar, curry paste, fish sauce, lime zest, lime juice, and basil in a large bowl.

3 Slice the chicken into thin strips, about ¼ inch wide. Stir the strips into the curry mixture, tossing until the chicken is coated. Toss in the bell pepper and the onion.

4 Divide the riced cauliflower evenly in the center of each piece of foil. Divide the chicken mixture evenly on top of the cauliflower.

5 Fold the foil over the mixture and crimp the edges for tent-style packages. Cook for 25 minutes, until the vegetables are hot and the chicken is cooked through.

MEXICAN CHICKEN WITH BLACK BEANS AND PEPPERS

2 tablespoons olive oil

1 tablespoon chili powder

2 teaspoons ground cumin

1 teaspoon fine sea salt

½ teaspoon smoked paprika

¼ teaspoon freshly ground black pepper

1 (15-ounce) can black beans, rinsed and drained

1 red bell pepper, cut into strips

1 yellow or orange bell pepper, cut into strips

½ red onion, thinly sliced

1½ pounds boneless, skinless chicken breasts

2 cups cooked rice

Optional toppings: sliced avocado, sour cream

This richly spiced meal is easy, but you can make it even more so by using leftover rice. Make a little extra the next time you cook either white or brown long-grained rice and store in a plastic bag in the freezer. It tends to get a little dry, making it good for stir-fries and dishes where you want separate grains, not clumps. The drier rice is good for soaking up the seasoned liquid that occurs when cooking chicken and vegetables in foil. Don't try uncooked rice—there isn't enough liquid in the mixture, and you'll end up with some crunchy raw bits.

OVEN TEMPERATURE 375°F   **GRILL** MEDIUM HEAT
FOIL 4 SHEETS HEAVY-DUTY NONSTICK FOIL OR FOIL LIGHTLY COATED WITH COOKING SPRAY
SIZE 12" X 15"   **TENT-STYLE** PACKAGE   **SERVES** 4

---

1 Preheat the oven to 375°F or your grill to medium heat.

2 Combine the oil, chili powder, cumin, salt, paprika, and pepper in a large bowl. Add the beans, bell peppers, and onion, and toss to blend well.

3 Trim the chicken and slice into ¼-inch strips. Stir into the vegetable mixture until the chicken is coated with spices.

4 Spoon ½ cup of rice into the center of each piece of foil. Top evenly with the chicken mixture. Fold the foil over the chicken mixture and crimp the edges for tent-style packages. Cook for 25 minutes, until the chicken is cooked through. Serve with avocado and sour cream, if desired.

VARIATION Substitute 3 to 4 cups shredded rotisserie chicken for sliced raw breasts. Cook for 15 minutes, until thoroughly hot.

ORANGE-TARRAGON CHICKEN WITH CANDIED CARROTS

Although tarragon leaves are small, they pack a lot of flavor. The anise-licorice-scented spicy herb blends particularly well with chicken and carrots, but take care to use only a small amount to avoid overpowering the dish.

×

OVEN TEMPERATURE 350°F   **GRILL** MEDIUM HEAT
FOIL 4 SHEETS NONSTICK FOIL OR
FOIL LIGHTLY COATED WITH COOKING SPRAY
SIZE 12" X 18"   **TENT-STYLE** PACKAGE   **SERVES** 4

×

---

2 tablespoons butter

¼ cup firmly packed light brown sugar

½ teaspoon fresh tarragon leaves or ¼ teaspoon dried tarragon

¾ teaspoon fine sea salt

¼ teaspoon freshly ground black pepper

1 seedless orange

4 carrots, peeled and thinly sliced

1¼ pounds boneless, skinless chicken breasts, sliced

1 tablespoon chopped fresh chives

1 Preheat the oven to 350°F or your grill to medium heat.

2 Place the butter in a glass measuring cup or small bowl and microwave for 20 seconds, until melted. Combine the brown sugar, tarragon, salt, and pepper in a medium bowl. Stir in the melted butter. Grate the orange peel into the butter mixture and stir until blended. Stir in the carrots and chicken.

3 Cut the orange in half and then into ¼-inch-thick slices. Divide the orange slices and place evenly in the center of each piece of foil. Top the orange slices evenly with the chicken mixture. Sprinkle with the chives.

4 Fold the foil over the mixture and crimp the edges for tent-style packages. Cook for 30 minutes, until the carrots are tender and the chicken is cooked through.

TURKEY WITH SWEET POTATOES

2 tablespoons extra-virgin olive oil

1 tablespoon molasses

2 garlic cloves, minced

1 tablespoon fresh thyme leaves

1 teaspoon fine sea salt

¼ teaspoon freshly ground black pepper

2 sweet potatoes, peeled and cubed

⅓ cup roasted and salted pecan pieces or chopped pecans

4 (5- to 6-ounce) turkey breast cutlets

You can cut your own turkey cutlets from a large turkey breast. Make sure all the slices (and sweet potatoes) are the same thickness so the ingredients cook evenly. If some cutlets are larger than others, cut them into pieces and divide evenly.

OVEN TEMPERATURE 375°F **GRILL** MEDIUM HEAT
FOIL 4 SHEETS NONSTICK FOIL OR FOIL LIGHTLY COATED WITH COOKING SPRAY
SIZE 12" X 24" **TENT-STYLE** PACKAGE **SERVES** 4

---

1 Preheat the oven to 375°F or your grill to medium heat.

2 Combine the oil, molasses, garlic, thyme, salt, and pepper in a large bowl. Stir in the sweet potatoes and pecans. Spoon the sweet potato mixture evenly into the center of each piece of foil.

3 Divide the turkey cutlets evenly over the sweet potato mixture. Drizzle any seasoned liquid left in the bowl over the turkey.

4 Fold the foil over the vegetables and crimp the edges for tent-style packages. Cook for 35 minutes, until the turkey is cooked through and the vegetables are hot and tender.

STUFFED TURKEY CUTLETS

1 tablespoon butter, melted

1 (8-ounce) package cremini or button mushrooms

1 large shallot, minced

½ teaspoon fine sea salt

¼ teaspoon freshly ground black pepper

1 teaspoon poultry seasoning

1 tablespoon white wine (optional)

2 tablespoons chopped dried cranberries, apples, or apricots

2 slices bacon, cooked and chopped

2 tablespoons seasoned panko breadcrumbs

4 (4-ounce) turkey breast cutlets

There's no need to wait until November or to bake for hours to get the comforting taste of turkey. The filling looks dry when you roll up the cutlets but will moisten as the turkey cooks.

— ✕ —

OVEN TEMPERATURE 375°F   **GRILL** MEDIUM HEAT

FOIL 4 SHEETS NONSTICK FOIL OR FOIL LIGHTLY COATED WITH COOKING SPRAY

SIZE 12" X 12"   **TENT-STYLE** PACKAGE   **SERVES** 4

— ✕ —

1 Preheat the oven to 375°F or your grill to medium heat.

2 Melt the butter in a large skillet over medium heat. Add the mushrooms, shallot, salt, pepper, and poultry seasoning. Stir in the wine, if desired. Cook, stirring frequently, for 5 minutes, until the mushrooms are tender. Stir in the cranberries, bacon, and panko.

3 Place the turkey cutlets on a flat surface. Cover with a piece of plastic wrap and pound to a ¼-inch thickness. Divide the mushroom mixture evenly on top of the cutlets. Roll up the turkey and place a cutlet, seam side down, in the center of each piece of foil.

4 Fold the foil over the turkey roll and crimp the edges for tent-style packages. Cook for 25 minutes, until the turkey is cooked through.

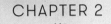

CHAPTER 2

CARNIVORE CRAVINGS

The granddaddy of all foil pack dinners is the hobo pack—a seasoned ground beef patty and a smattering of vegetables like onion, carrots, and potatoes.

Campers and Scouts have nailed this for decades, but there are many other delicious ways to cook beef and pork meals in foil.

Inexpensive and less marbled cuts of meat that are sliced or cubed are good options, since tougher cuts benefit from moist cooking methods. Save your expensive and exquisite T-bone, strips, and filet mignon for direct cooking on the grill and wrap up the vegetable sides instead.

Cuts from pork loin, like chops and tenderloin, are good candidates for foil packages since they tend to dry out with conventional cooking.

RECIBE LIST

RECIPE LIST

BASIC HOBO PACKET

2 red potatoes, sliced

1 cup baby carrots,
   quartered lengthwise

1 small onion, sliced

1 teaspoon Italian seasoning

½ teaspoon fine sea salt

¼ teaspoon freshly ground
   black pepper

1½ pounds lean ground beef

2 tablespoons
   Worcestershire sauce

1 tablespoon powdered
   steak seasoning blend
   or chili powder

The "hobo packet" is ground zero for foil pack dinners. There's no real trick for making this, but it's best if the potatoes and carrots are on the bottom, since they need the most heat. Any fat or seasoning in the meat will baste the vegetables, and you can vary the flavor by using different brands of steak seasoning.

— ✕ —

OVEN TEMPERATURE 350°F   **GRILL** MEDIUM HEAT
FOIL 4 SHEETS NONSTICK FOIL OR
FOIL LIGHTLY COATED WITH COOKING SPRAY
SIZE 12" X 18"   **TENT-STYLE** PACKAGE   **SERVES** 4

— ✕ —

1 Preheat the oven to 350°F or your grill to medium heat.

2 Divide the potatoes, carrots, and onion evenly and place in the center of each piece of foil. Sprinkle the vegetables evenly with Italian seasoning, salt, and pepper.

3 Combine the beef with the Worcestershire sauce and steak seasoning. Form the beef into 4 patties and place over the vegetables.

4 Fold the foil over the mixture and crimp the edges for tent-style packages. Cook for 40 minutes, until the vegetables are tender and the burger is cooked through.

ITALIAN MEATBALLS AND SAUCE

8 ounces uncooked pasta (optional)

½ pound ground turkey or chicken

½ pound hot Italian bulk sausage

¼ cup finely chopped onion

½ cup finely crushed saltine crackers

1 large egg

¼ cup grated Parmesan cheese

2 teaspoons Italian seasoning

½ teaspoon crushed red pepper flakes

2 cups marinara or spaghetti sauce

Shredded Parmesan cheese, to taste

Serve these zesty sauced meatballs over pasta, or spoon into hoagie rolls for a hearty sandwich. Whten cooked with the meatballs and sauce, the pasta soaks up extra liquid, making it very flavorful. Sprinkle with Parmesan cheese just before serving, and enjoy!

OVEN TEMPERATURE 375°F   **GRILL** MEDIUM HEAT
FOIL 4 SHEETS NONSTICK FOIL OR FOIL LIGHTLY COATED WITH COOKING SPRAY
SIZE 12" X 18"   **TENT-STYLE** PACKAGE   **SERVES** 4

---

1 If using, cook the pasta in boiling water to cover, according to the package directions. Drain and cover until ready to assemble the packages.

2 Preheat the oven to 375°F or your grill to medium heat.

3 Combine the ground turkey, sausage, onion, cracker crumbs, egg, cheese, seasoning, and red pepper flakes. Shape the beef mixture into 24 meatballs.

4 For the pasta, divide the cooked noodles evenly and place in the center of each piece of foil. Top the pasta with ½ cup marinara sauce. For sandwiches, spoon ½ cup sauce into the center of each piece of foil. Top each piece with 6 meatballs.

5 Fold the foil over the meatballs and crimp the edges for tent-style packages. Cook for 35 minutes, until the meatballs are cooked through.

EASY MEATLOAF

1 large egg

⅓ cup Molasses BBQ Sauce (recipe opposite) or store-bought smoky-flavored barbecue sauce

1 small onion, finely chopped

1½ pounds lean ground beef

1 cup panko breadcrumbs or crushed saltine crackers

1 Yukon gold or small russet potato, sliced

Adding barbecue sauce to ground beef adds flavor and moisture. This recipe doesn't include the traditional topping of sauce on the meatloaf because it could actually add *too* much moisture during cooking. If you like the extra flavor, drizzle some after cooking. If baking, you could open the foil packages and broil 1 or 2 minutes to caramelize the sauce.

×

OVEN TEMPERATURE 375°F   **GRILL** MEDIUM HEAT
FOIL 4 SHEETS NONSTICK FOIL OR
FOIL LIGHTLY COATED WITH COOKING SPRAY
SIZE 12" X 18"   **TENT-STYLE** PACKAGE   **SERVES** 6

×
---

1 Preheat the oven to 375°F or your grill to medium heat.

2 Beat the egg in a large bowl. Stir in the barbecue sauce, onion, beef, and crumbs. Form the beef mixture into 4 flat rectangles, about 1½ inches thick.

3 Divide the potato slices evenly in a single layer in the center of each piece of foil. Place a beef patty over the potatoes.

4 Fold the foil over the patties and crimp the edges for tent-style packages. Cook for 40 minutes, until the beef is hot and cooked through. Serve with additional sauce, if desired.

MOLASSES BBQ SAUCE

½ cup ketchup

2 tablespoons Dijon mustard

2 tablespoons Worcestershire
   sauce

2 tablespoons molasses

1 tablespoon apple cider
   vinegar

1 teaspoon ground chili powder

½ teaspoon ground cumin

⅛ teaspoon ground cayenne
   pepper

1 teaspoon liquid smoke

Combine all the ingredients in a bowl, whisking until well blended. Store in an airtight container in the fridge for up to one week. MAKES ¾ CUP

STUFFED CABBAGE ROLLS

- 8 green cabbage leaves
- 2 large eggs
- 1 to 1¼ pounds lean ground beef
- 1 cup cooked white or brown rice
- ¼ cup panko breadcrumbs
- 1 small onion, finely chopped
- 2 cloves garlic, minced
- 1 teaspoon Italian seasoning
- 1 teaspoon fine sea salt
- ½ teaspoon freshly ground black pepper
- 1¼ cups marinara sauce

Peeling off cabbage leaves gets tricky because they tend to tear as they're removed. An easy method is to remove the core from the center of a head of cabbage and gently boil the entire head in water to cover for about 10 minutes. The outside of the cabbage will cook first, and the leaves will easily loosen. You can then cut the remaining cabbage into wedges and freeze for up to a month until ready to use in other dishes.

OVEN TEMPERATURE 350°F   **GRILL** MEDIUM HEAT
FOIL 4 SHEETS NONSTICK FOIL OR
FOIL LIGHTLY COATED WITH COOKING SPRAY
SIZE 12" X 18"   **TENT-STYLE** PACKAGE   **SERVES** 4

---

1 Remove the core from the cabbage and peel off 8 leaves. (If some leaves tear, remove a few extra leaves and layer them to "patch" the torn places.) Cook the cabbage leaves in boiling water for about 5 minutes, until tender. Drain the leaves well in a colander and set aside until they're cool enough to handle. Cut away the hard center rib from the base of each leaf.

2 Preheat the oven to 350°F or your grill to medium heat.

3 Stir together the eggs in a large bowl until beaten. Add the beef, rice, panko, onion, garlic, seasoning, salt, pepper, and ¼ cup of the marinara sauce.

4 Spoon about ½ cup of the beef mixture onto each cabbage leaf near the thick end. Roll up the cabbage leaves, tucking in the sides to enclose the filling. Place 2 rolls in the center of each piece of foil. Spoon ¼ cup of the marinara sauce over the top of the rolls on each foil piece.

5 Fold the foil over the mixture and crimp the edges for tent-style packages. Cook for 40 minutes, until hot and the filling is cooked.

BEEF BRISKET

1 (4- to 4½-pound) flat beef brisket

3 tablespoons Dijon mustard

2 tablespoons dark brown sugar

1 tablespoon Worcestershire sauce

1 teaspoon liquid smoke

2 tablespoons paprika

1 tablespoon ground cumin

1 tablespoon ground chili powder

1 tablespoon kosher salt

2 teaspoons freshly ground black pepper

2 teaspoons garlic powder

2 teaspoons ground celery seed

Briskets are large cuts of beef that are often divided and sold as either a lean flat cut or fattier point cut. The key to fall-apart brisket is cooking it "low and slow."

×

OVEN TEMPERATURE 300°F   **GRILL** MEDIUM-LOW, INDIRECT HEAT (PAGE 4)
FOIL 1 TO 3 SHEETS HEAVY-DUTY FOIL
SIZE 12" X 24" OR LARGER   **FLAT** PACKAGE   **SERVES** 6 TO 8

×
---

1 Trim away the outer layer of fat on the brisket so that no more than ⅛ to ¼ inch remains.

2 Combine the mustard, brown sugar, Worcestershire sauce, and liquid smoke and spread over both sides of the brisket. Combine the paprika, cumin, chili powder, salt, pepper, garlic powder, and celery seed in a small bowl. Sprinkle the seasoning mix over all sides of the meat. Cover and marinate in the refrigerator for 4 hours or overnight. Remove the brisket from the refrigerator about an hour before cooking.

3 Preheat the oven to 300°F or prepare your grill for indirect heat.

4 Combine pieces of aluminum foil to create a piece large enough to completely cover the brisket. Use a double thickness on the bottom. Drain away excess marinade from the brisket and place the meat, fat side up, in the center of the foil. Fold the foil over the brisket and crimp the edges for a flat package.

5 Cook for 3 hours for a 4-pound roast (add 1 hour for each additional pound of beef). The brisket is done when the meat is fork-tender and the center of the meat registers 200°F. Remove the brisket from the oven and open the foil. Let rest for 20 to 30 minutes before slicing.

BRISKET WITH CORN PUDDING

1 (7- or 8-ounce) package cornbread or corn muffin mix

1 (14.75-ounce) can cream-style corn, undrained

1 (4-ounce) can diced green chilies, drained

1 (2-ounce) jar diced pimientos or 1 tablespoon chopped roasted red bell pepper

2 tablespoons butter, melted

1 teaspoon chili powder

½ teaspoon ground cumin

1 large egg

½ cup shredded cheddar cheese

1 cup chopped or shredded cooked brisket

Use leftovers and pantry ingredients to make this easy dinner any night. Just about any cooked protein would be delicious. Try it with grilled chicken or steak, or go vegetarian by adding a can of rinsed and drained black beans.

OVEN TEMPERATURE 375°F   **GRILL** MEDIUM HEAT

FOIL 4 SHEETS HEAVY-DUTY NONSTICK FOIL OR FOIL LIGHTLY COATED WITH COOKING SPRAY

SIZE 12" X 15"   **TENT-STYLE** PACKAGE   **SERVES** 4

---

1 Preheat the oven to 375°F or your grill to medium heat.

2 Combine the cornbread mix, corn, chilies, pimientos, butter, chili powder, cumin, egg, cheese, and brisket in a large bowl. Spoon the mixture evenly into the center of each piece of foil.

3 Fold the foil over the mixture and crimp the edges for tent-style packages. Cook for 25 to 30 minutes, until hot and cooked through.

COWBOY BEEF AND BEAN CHILI

2 tablespoons ancho or
  plain chili powder

1 tablespoon ground cumin

2 teaspoons smoked paprika

¾ teaspoon fine sea salt

¼ teaspoon freshly ground
  black pepper

1¼ pounds cubed beef
  sirloin or shredded brisket

½ onion, chopped

2 garlic cloves, minced

1 (15.5-ounce) can diced
  fire-roasted or chili-
  seasoned tomatoes,
  well drained

1 (15.5-ounce) can pinto
  beans, rinsed and drained

Toppings: sour cream,
  shredded cheddar
  cheese, fresh cilantro

This hearty beef chili uses lean cubed beef, but you can substitute cooked shredded brisket for a different texture. Spoon over a square of cornbread, or serve with corn chips.

OVEN TEMPERATURE 350°F   **GRILL** MEDIUM HEAT
FOIL 4 SHEETS NONSTICK FOIL OR
FOIL LIGHTLY COATED WITH COOKING SPRAY
SIZE 12" X 18"   **TENT-STYLE** PACKAGE   **SERVES** 4

1 Preheat the oven to 350°F or your grill to medium heat.

2 Combine the chili powder, cumin, paprika, salt, and pepper in a large bowl. Add the beef, stirring until well coated. Stir in the onion, garlic, tomatoes, and beans.

3 Spoon the beef and bean mixture evenly onto each piece of foil. Fold the foil over the chili mixture and crimp the edges for tent-style packages. Cook for 35 minutes, until the beef is hot and cooked through. Serve the chili with toppings and cornbread, if desired.

IRISH BEEF STEW

½ cup dark beer

2 tablespoons tomato paste

1 tablespoon Worcestershire sauce

2 teaspoons beef bouillon granules

1 tablespoon cornstarch (optional)

1 teaspoon fresh thyme

1 teaspoon chopped fresh rosemary

½ teaspoon fine sea salt

¼ teaspoon freshly ground black pepper

1¼ pounds chuck or sirloin, cubed

3 carrots or parsnips, peeled and chopped

2 red potatoes, cubed

½ large onion, coarsely chopped

2 garlic cloves, minced

Dark beer adds an interesting flavor to this quick stew, and you can substitute red or white wine, if desired. Liquid from the cooking vegetables dissolves the bouillon, creating a flavorful broth. The cornstarch is optional, but it helps to thicken the sauce so it coats the meat and veggies.

✕

OVEN TEMPERATURE 350°F   **GRILL** MEDIUM HEAT
FOIL 4 SHEETS HEAVY-DUTY NONSTICK FOIL OR FOIL LIGHTLY COATED WITH COOKING SPRAY
SIZE 12" X 18"   **TENT-STYLE** PACKAGE   **SERVES** 4

✕
---

1 Preheat the oven to 350°F or your grill to medium heat.

2 Combine the beer, tomato paste, Worcestershire sauce, bouillon, cornstarch (if using), thyme, rosemary, salt, and pepper in a large bowl. Whisk together until the ingredients are well blended.

3 Stir in the beef, carrots, potatoes, onion, and garlic.

4 Divide the beef mixture evenly and place in the center of each piece of foil. Fold the foil over the stew mixture and crimp the edges for tent-style packages. Cook for 45 minutes, until the beef and vegetables are hot and tender.

CHUTNEY GLAZED PORK CHOPS

½ cup uncooked couscous

½ cup water

½ cup mango chutney

1 tablespoon butter, softened

¼ teaspoon cracked black pepper

8 ounces *haricots verts* (slender green beans)

4 (1-inch-thick) boneless pork chops, trimmed

Pork chops are cut from the loin, one of the leanest pieces of meat. The lack of marbling and thin cuts mean chops are prone to dryness from overcooking. Foil pack cooking surrounds the pork chop in moisture, creating a tender dinner. If you prefer bone-in chops, increase cooking time by 5 minutes and adjust the size of the foil so it covers completely. Boneless smoked pork chops make a tasty variation, too.

OVEN TEMPERATURE 350°F **GRILL** MEDIUM HEAT
FOIL 4 SHEETS NONSTICK FOIL OR FOIL LIGHTLY COATED WITH COOKING SPRAY
SIZE 12" X 15" **TENT-STYLE** PACKAGE **SERVES** 4

---

1 Preheat the oven to 350°F or your grill to medium heat.

2 Combine the couscous and water in a bowl; let stand 5 minutes. Combine the chutney, butter, and pepper in a small bowl.

3 Divide the couscous evenly and place in the center of each piece of foil. Top with the beans and pork chops. Spoon the chutney sauce evenly over each chop.

4 Fold the foil over the pork chop bundles and crimp the edges for tent-style packages. Cook for 25 minutes, until the pork is cooked and vegetables are tender.

MOLASSES MARINATED WHOLE PORK TENDERLOIN

Molasses adds a full-bodied and almost smoky flavor to the marinade. This distinctive sweetener differs in intensity with light and dark varieties. For something milder, substitute honey. Letting cuts of meat rest after cooking allows the moisture exuded during cooking to be reabsorbed, resulting in a juicy and tender meal.

— × —

OVEN TEMPERATURE 350°F **GRILL** MEDIUM HEAT
FOIL 2 SHEETS HEAVY-DUTY NONSTICK FOIL OR FOIL LIGHTLY COATED WITH COOKING SPRAY
SIZE 12" X 24" **FLAT** PACKAGE **SERVES** 4

— × —

3 tablespoons unsulfured molasses

3 tablespoons apple cider vinegar

2 tablespoons soy sauce

1 tablespoon extra-virgin olive oil

2 teaspoons fresh thyme leaves

¼ teaspoon crushed red pepper flakes

1 (1- to 1½-pound) package pork tenderloin (2 per package), trimmed

1 Preheat the oven to 350°F or your grill to medium heat.

2 Combine the molasses, vinegar, soy sauce, oil, thyme, and pepper flakes in a large bowl or plastic storage bag.

3 Place the pork in the marinade, turning to coat. Cover or seal and refrigerate for several hours or overnight. Remove the pork from the marinade, discarding the liquid.

4 Place a tenderloin in the center of each piece of foil. Fold the foil over the pork and crimp the edges for a flat package. Cook for 35 minutes, until the pork reaches an internal temperature of 140°F. Let rest for 10 minutes before slicing.

PORK TENDERLOIN WITH APPLES AND ONIONS

Apples and onions are a natural pairing with pork tenderloin. In addition to adding flavor, they exude a lot of liquid during cooking, which can dilute other seasonings. The cider-mustard sauce is reduced before assembling, so it maintains its zest when blending with the apple and onion juices.

✕

OVEN TEMPERATURE 350°F   **GRILL** MEDIUM HEAT
FOIL 4 SHEETS HEAVY-DUTY NONSTICK FOIL OR FOIL LIGHTLY COATED WITH COOKING SPRAY
SIZE 12" X 18"   **TENT-STYLE** PACKAGE   **SERVES** 4

✕

¾ cup apple cider vinegar

½ cup packed light brown sugar

3 tablespoons whole-grain mustard

¼ teaspoon fine sea salt

¼ teaspoon freshly ground black pepper

1 large onion, halved and sliced

2 Granny Smith, Gala, or other crisp apples, peeled, cored, and sliced

1 (1- to 1½-pound) package pork tenderloin (2 per package), trimmed (see Note)

NOTE Before slicing the tenderloin, you'll need to trim away the "silver skin" from the top. Slip a sharp boning or chef's knife between the silver skin and meat. Glide the knife along the tenderloin, holding the silver skin up and away until completely removed.

1 Preheat the oven to 350°F or your grill to medium heat.

2 Combine the vinegar, brown sugar, mustard, salt, and pepper in a small saucepan. Bring to a boil over medium-high heat. Reduce the heat and simmer for 15 to 20 minutes, until thickened. Set aside.

3 Divide the onion and apple slices and place evenly in the center of each piece of foil. Slice the tenderloin into ¾-inch pieces; divide evenly and place over the onion and apples. Drizzle the mustard sauce over the pork mixture.

4 Fold the foil over the mixture and crimp the edges for tent-style packages. Cook for 25 minutes, until the pork is cooked through.

BABY BACK RIBS

1 tablespoon light brown sugar

1 teaspoon chili powder

½ teaspoon fine sea salt

½ teaspoon freshly ground black pepper

½ teaspoon garlic powder

¼ teaspoon ground cayenne pepper

1 (2½-pound) package baby back ribs

Molasses BBQ Sauce (page 53)

Double-wrap the rib bundles in foil to help prevent leaking as they are periodically turned over. To protect your oven from spills, cook on a baking sheet. For easy cleanup, line the baking sheet with foil, too.

———————— ✕ ————————

OVEN TEMPERATURE 325°F   **GRILL** MEDIUM-LOW HEAT
FOIL 8 SHEETS NONSTICK FOIL OR
FOIL LIGHTLY COATED WITH COOKING SPRAY
SIZE 12" X 18"   **FLAT** PACKAGE   **SERVES** 4

———————— ✕ ————————

1 Preheat the oven to 325°F or your grill to medium-low heat.

2 Stir together the brown sugar, chili powder, salt, pepper, garlic powder, and cayenne in a small bowl.

3 Remove the membrane from the back of the ribs by cutting a small piece loose with a sharp knife. Grab the membrane with a paper towel for a better grip and pull off. Cut the rack(s) of ribs into 4 portions, about 3 or 4 ribs each.

4 Sprinkle the seasoning blend on all sides of the ribs. Place each portion in the center of two pieces of foil stacked on top of each other. Fold the foil over the mixture and crimp the edges for flat packages. If you're baking in the oven, place the foil packages on a baking sheet. Cook for 60 minutes, turning over occasionally, until the ribs are tender.

5 If baking, open the foil and turn the ribs bone-side down. Brush the ribs with a few tablespoons of the sauce. Broil for 5 minutes, until the sauce is bubbly and the exterior is crisp. If grilling, remove from the foil. Baste the ribs with a few tablespoons of the sauce. Grill, bone-side down, for 5 to 10 minutes, until the sauce is bubbly. Serve the ribs with the remaining sauce on the side.

HAM, HASH BROWN, AND EGG BAKE

6 large eggs

½ cup half and half
or whipping cream

1 teaspoon seasoned salt

1 teaspoon fresh thyme
leaves plus additional for
garnish, if desired

¼ teaspoon freshly ground
black pepper

1 (20-ounce) package
refrigerated plain or
seasoned shredded hash
browns

1 cup chopped smoked ham
or cooked and crumbled
sausage

2 cups (8 ounces) shredded
Pepper Jack or cheddar
cheese

6 slices whole-wheat bread

Hot sauce (optional)

Reminiscent of the ubiquitous hash brown casseroles served at gatherings of family and friends, this version takes the same flavors and makes them single-serve. Use nonstick foil or ensure the entire sheet of foil is lightly greased to avoid sticking. If you like crispy hash browns, you'll need to sauté them before assembling—more work, but really tasty!

—————————— ✕ ——————————

OVEN TEMPERATURE 375°F   **GRILL** MEDIUM HEAT
FOIL 6 SHEETS NONSTICK FOIL OR
FOIL LIGHTLY COATED WITH COOKING SPRAY
SIZE 12" X 18"   **TENT-STYLE** PACKAGE   **SERVES** 6

—————————— ✕ ——————————

1 Preheat the oven to 375°F or your grill to medium heat.

2 Whisk together the eggs, half and half, salt, thyme, and pepper in a large bowl.

3 Stir in the hash browns, ham, and half of the cheese. Place one slice of bread in the center of each piece of foil. Spoon the egg mixture evenly onto each piece of bread. Sprinkle evenly with the remaining cheese.

4 Fold the foil over the mixture and crimp the edges for tent-style packages. Cook for 40 minutes, until cooked through. Garnish with fresh thyme and serve with hot sauce, if desired.

HONEY-MUSTARD HAM WITH POTATOES AND GREEN BEANS

2 tablespoons mayonnaise

1 tablespoon whole-grain mustard

1 tablespoon honey

2 teaspoons apple cider vinegar

¼ teaspoon fine sea salt

⅛ teaspoon freshly ground black pepper

1 large red potato, cubed

8 ounces *haricots verts* (slender green beans)

1 (8-ounce) ham steak

It doesn't take long to warm the cooked ham, but it's important to heat the packages long enough to fully cook the potatoes and green beans. *Haricot vert* is the French term for green bean, but it usually means a very slender green bean.

OVEN TEMPERATURE 350°F **GRILL** MEDIUM HEAT
FOIL 2 SHEETS NONSTICK FOIL OR FOIL LIGHTLY COATED WITH COOKING SPRAY
SIZE 12" X 15" **TENT-STYLE** PACKAGE **SERVES** 2

1 Preheat the oven to 350°F or your grill to medium heat.

2 Stir together the mayonnaise, mustard, honey, vinegar, salt, and pepper in a large bowl. Add the potato and beans, stirring until the vegetables are coated. Divide the vegetables evenly in the center of each piece of foil.

3 Slice the ham steak in half and place it over the vegetables. Drizzle any seasoned liquid from the bowl over the ham steaks.

4 Fold the foil over the mixture and crimp the edges for tent-style packages. Cook for 35 minutes, until the ham is cooked and the vegetables are tender.

HAM AND BRUSSELS AU GRATIN

1 pound Brussels sprouts, trimmed and halved or quartered

3 tablespoons butter, melted

½ cup heavy whipping cream

1 cup (4 ounces) shredded Gouda cheese

¼ cup grated Parmesan cheese

½ teaspoon fine sea salt

¼ teaspoon freshly ground black pepper

4 ounces ham steak or thickly sliced deli ham, chopped

The small shape of Brussels sprouts may look adorable, but they're packed with nutrition and flavor. Choose smaller ones—they're sweeter and cook quickly. If you prefer very soft Brussels sprouts, boil them for 15 minutes before assembling.

OVEN TEMPERATURE 350°F   **GRILL** MEDIUM HEAT
FOIL 4 SHEETS HEAVY-DUTY NONSTICK FOIL OR FOIL LIGHTLY COATED WITH COOKING SPRAY
SIZE 12" X 18"   **TENT-STYLE** PACKAGE   **SERVES** 2

---

1 Preheat the oven to 350°F or your grill to medium heat.

2 Cook the Brussels sprouts in boiling water to cover for 10 minutes; drain well.

3 Combine the butter, cream, cheeses, salt, and pepper in a large bowl. Stir in the Brussels sprouts and ham. Divide the mixture evenly in the center of each piece of foil.

4 Fold the foil over the mixture and crimp the edges for tent-style packages. Cook for 25 to 30 minutes, until the vegetables are tender and the mixture is hot and bubbly.

SMOKED PORK CHOP, SWEET POTATO, AND CRANBERRY BAKE

2 (4-ounce) smoked pork chops or 1 (8-ounce) ham steak, cut in half

1 large sweet potato, peeled and cubed

¼ cup dried cranberries

2 tablespoons butter, melted

⅓ cup packed light brown sugar

½ teaspoon ground cinnamon

½ teaspoon allspice

¼ teaspoon fine sea salt

Sweet potatoes and cranberries are a match made in fall heaven, especially when scented with cinnamon and allspice.

×

OVEN TEMPERATURE 350°F   **GRILL** MEDIUM HEAT
FOIL 4 SHEETS HEAVY-DUTY NONSTICK FOIL OR FOIL LIGHTLY COATED WITH COOKING SPRAY
SIZE 12" X 15"   **TENT-STYLE** PACKAGE   **SERVES** 2

×

1 Preheat the oven to 350°F or your grill to medium heat.

2 Place a pork chop in the center of each piece of foil. Divide the sweet potato and cranberries and place evenly over the pork chop.

3 Stir together butter, brown sugar, cinnamon, allspice, and salt. Drizzle over the pork and sweet potato mixture.

4 Fold the foil over the pork chop bundle and crimp the edges for tent-style packages. Cook for 20 minutes, until thoroughly heated.

PASTA CARBONARA WITH BLUE CHEESE AND WALNUTS

1 tablespoon butter, melted

½ cup heavy whipping cream

1 egg yolk

¼ cup shredded Parmesan cheese

¼ cup crumbled blue or shredded mozzarella cheese

4 slices pancetta or bacon, cooked and crumbled

4 ounces spaghetti or linguine, cooked

¼ cup chopped toasted walnuts

Make this rich and flavorful pasta dish heartier by stirring in a cup of shredded or chopped rotisserie chicken. Blue cheese isn't typically added to carbonara dishes but adds a bold twist. Use the same amount of Parmesan if you want to substitute.

OVEN TEMPERATURE 325°F   **GRILL** MEDIUM-LOW HEAT
FOIL 4 SHEETS HEAVY-DUTY NONSTICK FOIL OR FOIL LIGHTLY COATED WITH COOKING SPRAY
SIZE 12" X 18"   **TENT-STYLE** PACKAGE   **SERVES** 2

---

1 Preheat the oven to 325°F or your grill to medium-low heat.

2 Combine the butter, cream, egg yolk, Parmesan, blue cheese, and pancetta in a large bowl. Add the pasta and walnuts, stirring until the pasta mixture is coated.

3 Divide the mixture evenly on the foil sheets. Fold the foil over the mixture and crimp the edges for tent-style packages. Cook for 30 minutes, until the mixture is hot and bubbly.

SMOKED SAUSAGE OVER HERBED POLENTA

3 cups chicken or vegetable broth

1 teaspoon dried Italian seasoning

½ teaspoon fine sea salt

1 cup polenta or yellow cornmeal

2 tablespoons butter

1 (12-ounce) package smoked sausage, sliced

2 yellow, red, or orange bell peppers, thinly sliced

½ large sweet onion, sliced

Polenta is basically cornmeal boiled to create a porridge. Generally, polenta might become soft enough to eat in half the cooking time listed on the package, but longer heat makes it creamier and more tender. You'll find coarse-ground varieties that make a heartier texture; if you use instant polenta, watch the cooking time, since it's done in less than half the time and might require different amounts of liquid. Adjust the amount of liquid based on the package's directions. Southerners may prefer stone-ground grits; they work equally well.

✕

OVEN TEMPERATURE 375°F   **GRILL** MEDIUM HEAT
FOIL 4 SHEETS HEAVY-DUTY NONSTICK FOIL OR FOIL LIGHTLY COATED WITH COOKING SPRAY
SIZE 12" X 18"   **TENT-STYLE** PACKAGE   **SERVES** 4

✕

1 Preheat the oven to 375°F or your grill to medium heat.

2 Combine the broth, seasoning, and salt in a medium saucepan and bring to a boil. Whisk in the polenta gradually. Reduce the heat to low and simmer, stirring frequently, for 20 to 25 minutes, until tender. Stir in the butter. (The mixture will pop and sputter like lava, so put a lid over the top, leaving space for steam to escape.)

3 Spoon the mixture evenly into the center of each foil piece. Top evenly with the sausage, bell peppers, and onion.

4 Fold the foil over the mixture and crimp the edges for tent-style packages. Cook for 25 to 30 minutes, until hot.

BRATS WITH APPLES AND SAUERKRAUT

1 (16-ounce) package refrigerated sauerkraut, drained

1 large apple, cored and cut into thin wedges

½ green bell pepper, chopped

½ onion, thinly sliced

3 tablespoons light brown sugar

¼ cup whole-grain mustard

1 (16-ounce) package (4) bratwurst sausages

Hot dog or hoagie buns

Brat, short for bratwurst, is a German-style sausage. It's usually already cooked and only needs reheating. If you use an uncooked version, add 10 minutes to your cooking time to ensure the sausage is completely done.

×

OVEN TEMPERATURE 375°F   **GRILL** MEDIUM HEAT
FOIL 4 SHEETS HEAVY-DUTY FOIL
SIZE 12" X 18"   **TENT-STYLE** PACKAGE   **SERVES** 4

×

1 Preheat the oven to 375°F or your grill to medium heat.

2 Combine the sauerkraut, apple, bell pepper, onion, brown sugar, and mustard in a large bowl. Stir until well blended.

3 Spoon the sauerkraut mixture evenly into the center of each piece of foil. Slice the sausages in half lengthwise and place on top of the sauerkraut.

4 Fold the foil over the mixture and crimp the edges for tent-style packages. Cook for 25 minutes, until hot.

CHAPTER 3

×

CATCH OF THE DAY

If any protein were designed specifically for foil packet cooking, it's a fish fillet.

Quick-cooking seafood benefits from the moisture held within a pouch. As the ingredients all steam together, the seafood is bathed in flavor. Neutral or mild fish greatly benefits from high-flavor additions like olives or lemons. You can still create daring combinations by pairing bold-flavored fish (like salmon) with adventurous elements without over-whelming the seafood.

Fish and shellfish are healthy choices, but their vulnerability is their leanness. Include a splash of healthy oil and ingredients that add moisture, like citrus and summer squash, and you'll create delicious and moist meals.

RECEIPE LIST

— ✕ —

BOURBON AND BACON SHRIMP

⅓ cup pepper jelly

1 tablespoon butter, melted

⅓ cup Molasses BBQ Sauce (page 53) or store-bought barbecue sauce

1 tablespoon bourbon

1½ pounds large shrimp, peeled and deveined

6 slices bacon, cooked and coarsely chopped

Eat these spicy and saucy shrimp as is, or spoon the mixture over cooked rice, pasta, or baked potatoes. Remember to use indirect heat if you are grilling, since hot spots might scorch the pepper jelly.

———————————— ✕ ————————————

OVEN TEMPERATURE 350°F   **GRILL** MEDIUM, INDIRECT HEAT (PAGE 4)
FOIL 4 SHEETS NONSTICK FOIL OR FOIL LIGHTLY COATED WITH COOKING SPRAY
SIZE 12" X 15"   **TENT-STYLE** PACKAGE   **SERVES** 4

———————————— ✕ ————————————

1 Preheat the oven to 350°F or your grill to medium heat.

2 Combine the pepper jelly and butter in a 2-cup glass measuring cup. Microwave for 30 to 60 seconds on high heat, until the butter and jelly melt; stir to combine. Stir in the barbecue sauce and bourbon.

3 Toss the shrimp and bacon in the sauce and spoon evenly into the center of each piece of foil. Fold the foil and crimp the edges for tent-style packages. If baking in the oven, place the packages on a baking sheet.

4 Cook for 15 minutes, until the shrimp are done and the sauce is bubbly.

LOUISIANA-STYLE BBQ SHRIMP

½ cup (1 stick) butter

3 tablespoons Worcestershire sauce

1 tablespoon Creole or Cajun seasoning blend

3 garlic cloves, minced

2 pounds large shrimp

2 lemons, sliced

1 small sweet onion, quartered and sliced

French bread

This New Orleans shrimp dish doesn't use traditional tomato-based barbecue sauce, regardless of the name. Instead, the shrimp are basted in butter sauce flavored with garlic, onion, and Worcestershire. You'll want a lot of extra bread to sop up every bit of flavorful liquid. Unpeeled shrimp will add more seafood flavor, but if you want to avoid the mess of peeling, go ahead and do that before assembling.

✕

OVEN TEMPERATURE 350°F **GRILL** MEDIUM, INDIRECT HEAT (PAGE 4)

FOIL 4 SHEETS HEAVY-DUTY FOIL

SIZE 12" X 24" **TENT-STYLE** PACKAGE **SERVES** 4

✕

1 Preheat the oven to 350°F or your grill to medium, indirect heat.

2 Heat the butter in a glass or ceramic bowl in the microwave for 30 to 60 seconds, until melted. Stir in the Worcestershire, seasoning, and garlic.

3 Combine the shrimp, lemons, and onion in a large bowl. Add the butter mixture, stirring until the ingredients are well coated. Spoon the shrimp mixture into the center of each piece of foil. Drizzle the remaining butter mixture evenly over the shrimp.

4 Fold the foil over the mixture and crimp the edges for tent-style packages. If baking, place the packages on a baking sheet. Cook for 15 minutes, until the shrimp are done. Serve with sliced French bread.

SHRIMP NACHOS

4 ounces cream cheese, softened

½ cup sour cream

2 teaspoons ground cumin

1 teaspoon seafood seasoning

1 bunch green onions, chopped

1 cup shredded Pepper Jack or Colby cheese

1 cup shredded cheddar cheese

1 pound cooked shrimp, peeled, deveined, and coarsely chopped

8 cups blue or yellow corn tortilla chips

⅓ cup sliced pickled jalapeño peppers

2 tablespoons chopped fresh cilantro

Seafood lovers will enjoy noshing on this as a snack or light entrée. It's flexible enough to add other ingredients, such as a cup of lump crab or cooked black beans. Don't go overboard or you'll overpower the delicate flavor of the seafood. If you enjoy pico de gallo or salsa with your nachos, you can serve them on the side.

×

OVEN TEMPERATURE 325°F   **GRILL** MEDIUM-LOW HEAT
FOIL 4 SHEETS HEAVY-DUTY NONSTICK FOIL OR FOIL LIGHTLY COATED WITH COOKING SPRAY
SIZE 12" X 24"   **TENT-STYLE** PACKAGE   **SERVES** 4

×

1 Preheat the oven to 325°F or your grill to medium-low heat.

2 Combine the cream cheese, sour cream, cumin, seafood seasoning, green onions, and cheeses in a large bowl. Stir in the shrimp.

3 Divide the tortilla chips and place in the center of each piece of foil. Top evenly with the seafood mixture. Sprinkle with the jalapeño peppers.

4 Fold the foil over the seafood mixture and crimp the edges for tent-style packages. Cook for 15 minutes, until the nachos are hot and the cheese is melted. Sprinkle each serving evenly with the cilantro.

SHRIMP BOIL IN FOIL

8 baby red potatoes, halved if large

1 large ear of corn, sliced into 1-inch pieces

½ small onion, cut into wedges

6 ounces smoked sausage, sliced

1 pound large shrimp, peeled and deveined

1 lemon, cut into wedges

2 tablespoons butter, cut into small pieces

2 to 3 teaspoons seafood or Cajun-blend seasoning

The key to making this simple dinner a success is to make sure there is ample room in the foil packages for the ingredients to steam. Since the potatoes will take the longest to cook, give them a head start in the microwave to make sure they are tender and cooked through when the quick-cooking shrimp are done.

OVEN TEMPERATURE 350°F   **GRILL** MEDIUM HEAT
FOIL 2 SHEETS HEAVY-DUTY NONSTICK FOIL OR FOIL LIGHTLY COATED WITH COOKING SPRAY
SIZE 12" X 24"   **TENT-STYLE** PACKAGE   **SERVES** 2

---

1 Preheat the oven to 350°F or your grill to medium heat.

2 Place the potatoes in a glass or ceramic dish and add about ¼ cup water. Cover with plastic wrap and microwave for 2 minutes. Drain well.

3 Place the potatoes, corn, onion, sausage, shrimp, and lemon wedges evenly in the center of each piece of foil. Sprinkle evenly with the butter pieces and seasoning.

4 Fold the foil over the mixture and crimp the edges for tent-style packages. Cook for 20 minutes, until the potatoes are tender and the shrimp are done. Sprinkle with additional seafood seasoning, if you wish.

SEAFOOD AND SAUSAGE JAMBALAYA

½ large onion, finely chopped

1 green bell pepper, finely chopped

2 celery stalks, finely chopped

2 garlic cloves, minced

1 (15.5-ounce) can diced tomatoes, drained

4 green onions, chopped

2 tablespoons extra-virgin olive oil

1 tablespoon Creole seasoning blend

½ teaspoon dried thyme

½ teaspoon dried oregano

3 cups cooked long-grain white rice

1 pound shrimp, peeled and deveined

1 (12-ounce) package smoked or cooked andouille sausage, sliced

Many jambalaya recipes start with uncooked rice, adding enough seasoned liquid so the grains cook up tender and flavorful. The amount of liquid necessary to cook the rice could easily leak out of foil pouches, so this recipe uses cooked rice as a shortcut. This is a great way to use leftover rice. For maximum flavor, cook the rice in broth.

✕

OVEN TEMPERATURE 375°F   **GRILL** MEDIUM HEAT
FOIL 4 SHEETS NONSTICK FOIL OR
FOIL LIGHTLY COATED WITH COOKING SPRAY
SIZE 12" X 18"   **TENT-STYLE** PACKAGE   **SERVES** 4

✕

1 Preheat the oven to 375°F or your grill to medium heat.

2 Combine the onion, bell pepper, celery, garlic, tomatoes, green onions, oil, Creole seasoning, thyme, and oregano in a large bowl. Add the rice, shrimp, and sausage, stirring until the mixture is well blended.

3 Spoon the mixture evenly into the center of each piece of foil. Fold the foil over the rice mixture and crimp the edges for tent-style packages. If baking, place the packages on a sheet pan. Cook for 30 minutes, until the shrimp are cooked through.

SCALLOPS ADOBO

1 tablespoon butter

1 tablespoon soy sauce

2 teaspoons tomato paste

2 teaspoons light brown sugar

2 teaspoons white wine vinegar

1 teaspoon ancho chili powder

⅛ teaspoon freshly ground black pepper

Pinch of ground cloves

6 large sea scallops

Microgreens or chopped fresh herbs (optional)

When shopping for this recipe, look for "dry-pack" scallops, which means they have not been stored in water or treated with preservatives that tend to make the scallops leach water excessively when cooked. Remove the "foot" on the side of each scallop. It's edible but tough.

OVEN TEMPERATURE 350°F   **GRILL** MEDIUM HEAT
FOIL 2 SHEETS NONSTICK FOIL OR
FOIL LIGHTLY COATED WITH COOKING SPRAY
SIZE 12" X 18"   **TENT-STYLE** PACKAGE   **SERVES** 2

---

1 Preheat the oven to 350°F or your grill to medium heat.

2 Heat the butter in a small bowl in the microwave for 20 to 30 seconds, until melted. Stir in the soy sauce, tomato paste, brown sugar, vinegar, chili powder, black pepper, and cloves.

3 Toss the scallops with the butter mixture until coated on all sides. Spoon the scallops evenly into the center of each piece of foil. Drizzle any leftover liquid evenly over the scallops.

4 Fold the foil over the scallops and crimp the edges for tent-style packages. Cook for 15 minutes, until the scallops are cooked. Garnish with microgreens or fresh herbs, if desired.

GRILLED GARLIC MUSSELS

2 pounds mussels, scrubbed

¼ cup chopped fresh
    parsley

3 slices pancetta or
    prosciutto, chopped

2 garlic cloves, sliced

1 teaspoon orange zest

½ cup white wine

4 teaspoons butter

4 grilled bread slices

Steaming mussels (or clams, too) in foil is a fantastic and easy way to prepare this shellfish, since the enclosed space keeps the small, tender meat moist and succulent. Mussels will exude plenty of liquid that will marry with the seasoning ingredients to make an irresistible dipping sauce. It's important that the pouches are well sealed to keep the ample liquid from oozing out. If in doubt, double-layer the foil or place the pouches on a baking sheet.

OVEN TEMPERATURE 425°F   **GRILL** MEDIUM-HIGH HEAT
FOIL 4 SHEETS HEAVY-DUTY FOIL
SIZE 12" X 24"   **TENT-STYLE** PACKAGE   **SERVES** 4

---

1 Preheat the oven to 425°F or your grill to medium-high heat. If using a baking sheet, place it in the oven to preheat.

2 Place the mussels evenly in the center of each piece of foil. Fold the sides together and crimp, leaving the top open. Sprinkle the parsley, pancetta, garlic, and orange zest evenly over the mussels. Drizzle evenly with the wine. Dot the butter evenly in each pouch.

3 Fold the foil and crimp the edges for tent-style packages. Cook for 6 to 8 minutes, until the mussels are cooked. Discard any mussels that do not open. Carefully pour the packages into a serving bowl, including the flavorful liquid. Serve with grilled bread for dipping.

SUPER SIMPLE WRAPPED FLOUNDER

4 (6-ounce) flounder, sole, or tilapia fillets

¼ cup toasted sliced or slivered almonds

2 tablespoons butter, cut into pieces

¼ teaspoon lemon zest

½ teaspoon fine sea salt

¼ teaspoon freshly ground black pepper

1 tablespoon chopped fresh parsley, chives, or basil

Lemon wedges

This easy seafood dinner is a riff on the classic whitefish amandine recipes you may see in classic French restaurants. Here, the flour coating is omitted, but the dish includes butter, lemon, and the crunchy almonds that make it a perennial favorite. The almonds are toasted in advance since they need dry heat to brown. Brown for 3 to 5 minutes in a toaster oven or buy them packaged in markets, usually near the salad toppings.

✕

OVEN TEMPERATURE 400°F   **GRILL** MEDIUM-HIGH HEAT
FOIL 4 SHEETS NONSTICK FOIL OR
FOIL LIGHTLY COATED WITH COOKING SPRAY
SIZE 12" X 18"   **TENT-STYLE** PACKAGE   **SERVES** 4

✕

1 Preheat the oven to 400°F or your grill to medium-high heat.

2 Place the fish fillets in the center of each piece of foil. Sprinkle the almonds, butter, lemon zest, salt, pepper, and parsley evenly over the fillets.

3 Fold the foil over the fish and crimp the edges to seal into tent-style packages. Cook for 10 minutes, until the fish is cooked through. Serve with lemon wedges.

SNAPPER VERACRUZ

Snapper is the traditional fish used in this spicy Mexican dish, but almost any fresh and firm fish fillet will taste equally delicious. The flavors are bold, so it's more about the sauce than the flavor of the seafood.

×

OVEN TEMPERATURE 350°F   **GRILL** MEDIUM HEAT

FOIL 4 SHEETS NONSTICK FOIL OR FOIL LIGHTLY COATED WITH COOKING SPRAY

SIZE 12" X 18"   **TENT-STYLE** PACKAGE   **SERVES** 4

×

- 3 large Roma or 1 large tomato, seeded and diced
- 2 jarred roasted red bell peppers, drained well and diced
- ½ cup pitted green olives, chopped
- ¼ large sweet onion, thinly sliced
- ¼ cup chopped fresh cilantro
- ¼ cup chopped fresh parsley
- 2 tablespoons pickled jalapeño, chopped
- 1 tablespoon extra-virgin olive oil
- 1½ teaspoons capers, rinsed and drained
- 4 (6-ounce) yellowtail snapper or other firm whitefish fillets

1 Preheat the oven to 350°F or your grill to medium heat.

2 Combine the tomato, bell peppers, olives, onion, cilantro, parsley, jalapeño, oil, and capers in a large bowl.

3 Place one snapper fillet in the center of each piece of foil. Top the fish evenly with the tomato mixture.

4 Fold the foil over the fish and crimp the edges for tent-style packages. Cook for 15 to 20 minutes, until thoroughly heated.

FLATFISH WITH SPICED COUSCOUS

1 cup cooked couscous

1 tablespoon extra-virgin olive oil

½ teaspoon lemon zest

1 tablespoon fresh lemon juice

1 teaspoon ground cumin

1 teaspoon chopped fresh mint

½ teaspoon fine sea salt

¼ teaspoon freshly ground black pepper

1 zucchini, halved and sliced

2 Roma tomatoes, sliced and seeded

4 (4-ounce) boneless, skinless tilapia or other flatfish fillets

The tiny grains of couscous absorb liquid and soften quickly, making it the fastest and simplest pasta to prepare. You can substitute any grain—rice, quinoa, farro, or barley.

— ✕ —

OVEN TEMPERATURE 350°F   **GRILL** MEDIUM HEAT
FOIL 2 SHEETS NONSTICK FOIL OR
FOIL LIGHTLY COATED WITH COOKING SPRAY
SIZE 12" X 15"   **TENT-STYLE** PACKAGE   **SERVES** 2

— ✕ —

1 Preheat the oven to 350°F or your grill to medium heat.

2 Combine the couscous, oil, lemon zest, lemon juice, cumin, mint, salt, and pepper in a large bowl. Divide the couscous in half and spoon into the center of each piece of foil. Top evenly with the zucchini and tomatoes. Place the fish over the vegetables.

3 Fold the foil over the fish and crimp the edges for tent-style packages. Cook for 15 minutes, until the fish and the couscous are cooked.

TOMATO-OLIVE FISH IN FOIL

¼ cup extra-virgin olive oil

1 garlic clove, minced

½ teaspoon fine sea salt

¼ teaspoon freshly ground black pepper

1 lemon

4 (6-ounce) boneless, skinless whitefish fillets

12 red or yellow cherry or grape tomatoes, halved

12 pitted Kalamata olives, halved

¼ cup lightly packed fresh basil leaves

Olive oil is a key ingredient in Mediterranean dishes, and you'll want to use a good quality extra-virgin oil here. If you let the oil mixture rest for a few hours in the refrigerator, you'll have an even more flavorful dish as the garlic will infuse throughout it.

OVEN TEMPERATURE 375°F   **GRILL** MEDIUM HEAT
FOIL 2 SHEETS NONSTICK FOIL OR FOIL LIGHTLY COATED WITH COOKING SPRAY
SIZE 12" X 15"   **TENT-STYLE** PACKAGE   **SERVES** 4

---

1 Preheat the oven to 375°F or your grill to medium heat.

2 Combine the oil, garlic, salt, and pepper in a small bowl, stirring until well blended. Grate ½ teaspoon of lemon rind into the oil mixture, stirring well. Refrigerate up to a day ahead.

3 Place the fish fillets in the center of each piece of foil. Drizzle the oil mixture over the top of each piece of fish. Top evenly with the tomatoes, olives, and basil.

4 Cut the grated lemon into wedges and squeeze the wedges over the fish.

5 Fold the foil over the mixture and crimp the edges for tent-style packages. Cook for 20 minutes, until the fish is cooked through.

BAKED SALMON WITH ORANGE AND HERBS

1 seedless orange

4 plum tomatoes, seeded and diced

1 large shallot, minced

1 tablespoon chopped fresh tarragon

1 tablespoon chopped fresh basil

1 tablespoon chopped fresh thyme

2 tablespoons extra-virgin olive oil

¾ teaspoon fine sea salt

½ teaspoon freshly ground black pepper

4 (4-ounce) boneless sockeye salmon fillets

There are five types of wild-caught Alaskan salmon. Though any will work with this recipe, sockeye and king are the most common ones you'll see as fillets in seafood markets. King fillets can be thick and might require a few extra minutes of heat to cook to your desired level of doneness.

✕

OVEN TEMPERATURE 350°F   **GRILL** MEDIUM HEAT
FOIL 4 SHEETS NONSTICK FOIL OR
FOIL LIGHTLY COATED WITH COOKING SPRAY
SIZE 12" X 15"   **TENT-STYLE** PACKAGE   **SERVES** 4

✕

1 Preheat the oven to 350°F or your grill to medium heat.

2 Grate 1 teaspoon of the orange rind into a large bowl. Peel the orange and cut into segments; place the segments into the bowl. Stir in the tomatoes, shallot, tarragon, basil, thyme, olive oil, salt, and pepper.

3 Place one salmon fillet in the center of each piece of foil. Spoon the tomato mixture evenly over the salmon.

4 Fold the foil over the salmon and crimp the edges for tent-style packages. Cook for 20 to 30 minutes, until the salmon is cooked to your desired degree of doneness (20 minutes will cook the salmon to medium; for well-done salmon, cook for 30 minutes).

BLACKBERRY-HOISIN SALMON

1 (6.5-ounce) container fresh blackberries

¼ cup hoisin sauce

1 small shallot, minced

4 (6-ounce) boneless sockeye salmon fillets

2 green onions, sliced

1 teaspoon sesame seeds

The sweet-salty sauce is robust and pairs nicely with a bold-flavored fish like salmon. Frozen berries can be substituted, but make sure they are completely thawed and drained on paper towels.

—————————————— ✕ ——————————————

OVEN TEMPERATURE 350°F   **GRILL** MEDIUM HEAT
FOIL 2 SHEETS HEAVY-DUTY NONSTICK FOIL OR FOIL LIGHTLY COATED WITH COOKING SPRAY
SIZE 12" X 15"   **TENT-STYLE** PACKAGE   **SERVES** 4

—————————————— ✕ ——————————————

1 Preheat the oven to 350°F or your grill to medium heat.

2 Combine the blackberries, hoisin sauce, and shallot in a large bowl. Stir the mixture together, mashing lightly with the back of a spoon to crush the berries.

3 Place a salmon fillet in the center of each piece of foil. Spread the blackberry mixture evenly on top of the fillets. Sprinkle with green onions and sesame seeds.

4 Fold the foil over the salmon and crimp the edges to seal into tent-style packages. Cook for 20 to 30 minutes, until the salmon is cooked to your desired degree of doneness (20 minutes will cook the salmon to medium, depending on its thickness; for well-done salmon, cook for 30 minutes).

SESAME SALMON AND ASPARAGUS

¼ cup packed light brown sugar

2 tablespoons toasted sesame oil

1 tablespoon soy sauce

½ teaspoon smoked paprika

1 (12-ounce) boneless sockeye salmon or Arctic char fillet, halved

1 cup cooked rice

½ pound thin fresh asparagus spears

1 teaspoon sesame seeds

Full-flavored seafood like salmon pairs well with other strong ingredients, like toasted sesame oil or soy sauce. Arctic char resembles (and is related to) salmon but has a milder and more delicate flavor. Smoked paprika adds depth, but you can use regular or sweet paprika if you wish.

✖

OVEN TEMPERATURE 375°F   **GRILL** MEDIUM HEAT
FOIL 2 SHEETS HEAVY-DUTY NONSTICK FOIL OR FOIL LIGHTLY COATED WITH COOKING SPRAY
SIZE 12" X 15"   **TENT-STYLE** PACKAGE   **SERVES** 2

✖
---

1 Preheat the oven to 375°F or your grill to medium heat.

2 Combine the brown sugar, oil, soy sauce, and paprika in a small shallow dish. Add the salmon or char, turning to coat.

3 Spoon the rice evenly into the center of each piece of foil. Place the asparagus in a single layer over the rice. Place the salmon or char on top of the asparagus and sprinkle with the sesame seeds.

4 Fold the foil over the fish and crimp the edges for tent-style packages. Cook for 20 to 30 minutes, until the salmon or char is cooked to your desired degree of doneness (20 minutes will cook the fish to medium, depending on its thickness; for well-done fish, cook for 30 minutes).

HERB TROUT IN FOIL

2 tablespoons butter,
  softened

2 small garlic cloves, minced

¼ teaspoon fine sea salt

⅛ teaspoon freshly ground
  black pepper

4 (6-ounce) trout fillets

¼ cup chopped mixed fresh
  herbs, such as rosemary,
  parsley, thyme, and/or
  chives

2 lemons, sliced

Trout is sold whole and filleted in markets. While 6 ounces is a typical weight for a serving, each fillet may weigh up to a pound or more. You can allow for a larger serving per person, adding a minute or two to the cooking time. As a general rule, fish cooks in 10 minutes per inch.

—————————————— ✕ ——————————————

OVEN TEMPERATURE 375°F   **GRILL** MEDIUM HEAT
FOIL 4 SHEETS NONSTICK FOIL OR
FOIL LIGHTLY COATED WITH COOKING SPRAY
SIZE 12" X 18"   **FLAT** PACKAGE   **SERVES** 4

—————————————— ✕ ——————————————

1 Preheat the oven to 375°F or your grill to medium heat.

2 Combine the butter, garlic, salt, and pepper in a small bowl. Spread the butter mixture over the top of the fillets. Place the fish, skin side down, in the center of each piece of foil.

3 Sprinkle the herbs evenly over the fish. Place the lemon slices over the herbs. Fold the foil over the fish and crimp the edges for flat packages. Cook for 5 minutes, turn over, and continue to cook for 5 additional minutes, until the fish is cooked through.

CHAPTER 4

HANDHELD

The humble sandwich has long been a mainstay for handheld meals since our childhoods.

You may grow out of simple PB&J or two-ingredient grilled cheese sandwiches, but the concept of flavorful fillings wrapped in tender bread is timeless. While it's perfectly acceptable to gnaw on a layered bundle of chilled deli meats, heating it takes the sandwich from utility grub to delicious eats. Expand your concept of sandwich to include fajitas, tacos, and "bunless" burgers, and these handheld meals easily satisfy.

Any sandwich with cooked meat can be cooked completely assembled in a bun. For food safety, cook raw ground beef, meats, and fish separately to ensure their complete doneness before assembling on bread or tortillas. The moistest burgers you'll ever eat are wrapped in foil. There may be a fair amount of liquid in the package after it cooks. Choosing a lean ground beef or pork helps eliminate any greasiness.

RECIMPE LIST

×

BUFFALO CHICKEN BREAD

1 (16-ounce) loaf Italian
or French bread

1 (8-ounce) package cream
cheese, softened

¼ cup mayonnaise

½ cup hot sauce

¼ teaspoon freshly ground
black pepper

1 cup (4 ounces) shredded
mozzarella cheese

½ (8-ounce) package
sharp cheddar cheese,
shredded

2 cups shredded rotisserie
or roasted chicken

3 green onions, thinly sliced

Blue cheese salad dressing
(optional)

This high-flavor dish is very rich, so consider it an appetizer unless you have a strong appetite. Reduce the hot sauce by half if you prefer a milder dish (it's okay to taste before cooking since the chicken is already cooked).

× ---

OVEN TEMPERATURE 375°F   **GRILL** MEDIUM HEAT
FOIL 1 SHEET HEAVY-DUTY NONSTICK FOIL OR
FOIL LIGHTLY COATED WITH COOKING SPRAY
SIZE 12" X 24"   **FLAT** PACKAGE   **SERVES** 6 TO 8

× ---

1 Preheat the oven to 375°F or your grill to medium heat.

2 Slice off the top one-fourth of the bread. Scoop out the inside of the bread, leaving a ½-inch shell. (Save the bread pieces for breadcrumbs or other uses.) Place the bottom half of the bread, cut side up, in the center of the piece of foil.

3 Combine the cream cheese, mayonnaise, hot sauce, and pepper in a large bowl. Stir until the mixture is smooth and well blended. Stir in the mozzarella, cheddar, and chicken.

4 Spoon the chicken mixture into the bottom of the loaf. Sprinkle with the green onions. Place the bread top over the chicken mixture.

5 Fold the foil over the mixture and crimp the edges for a flat package. Cook for 25 minutes, until hot and bubbly. Slice into portions and serve with the blue cheese dressing, if desired.

CHICKEN PARMESAN SUBS

2 (8- to 10-ounce) boneless, skinless chicken breasts

½ cup all-purpose flour

1 teaspoon paprika

½ teaspoon garlic powder

½ teaspoon fine sea salt

2 large eggs, beaten

¾ cup seasoned panko breadcrumbs

Vegetable oil

1 cup marinara sauce

½ cup shredded mozzarella cheese

½ cup shredded Parmesan cheese

4 hoagie or ciabatta buns, split

There's a bit more effort to breading and sautéing the chicken breasts for this sandwich, but homemade is a lot more tender and flavorful than frozen, breaded cutlets (though it's okay if you need to use that shortcut!). The good news is that you can make the cutlets a few hours to a day ahead.

OVEN TEMPERATURE 375°F   **GRILL** MEDIUM HEAT
FOIL 2 SHEETS NONSTICK FOIL OR FOIL LIGHTLY COATED WITH COOKING SPRAY
SIZE 12" X 18"   **TENT-STYLE** PACKAGE   **SERVES** 4

---

1 Slice the chicken breasts in half lengthwise, creating 4 cutlets. Place the chicken between pieces of plastic wrap and pound to an even thickness.

2 Combine the flour, paprika, garlic powder, and salt in a shallow bowl. Beat the eggs in a second shallow bowl. Place the panko in a third shallow bowl.

3 Dredge the chicken in the flour mixture, then dip in the egg mixture, letting any excess drip off. Dredge the chicken in the panko until evenly coated. Set aside.

4 Heat a ¼-inch layer of oil in a heavy skillet over medium-high heat. Cook the breaded chicken for 5 minutes on each side, until golden brown and cooked through.

5 Preheat the oven to 375°F or your grill to medium heat.

6 Place each piece of chicken in the center of each piece of foil. Top evenly with the sauce and sprinkle evenly with the cheeses.

7 Fold the foil over the chicken and crimp the edges for tent-style packages. Cook for 15 to 20 minutes, until the chicken is hot and the cheese melts. Serve in the hoagie or ciabatta buns.

CHIPOTLE-RANCH CHICKEN QUESADILLAS

Rotisserie chicken is possibly the greatest shortcut for busy cooks. An average bird yields 4 cups of both light and dark meat. If your leftovers don't yield 3 full cups, add some rinsed and drained black beans, corn, or roasted red bell peppers.

OVEN TEMPERATURE 425°F   **GRILL** MEDIUM-HIGH HEAT
FOIL 8 SHEETS HEAVY-DUTY NONSTICK FOIL OR FOIL LIGHTLY COATED WITH COOKING SPRAY
SIZE 12" X 12"   **FLAT** PACKAGE   **SERVES** 4

¼ cup buttermilk ranch salad dressing

2 teaspoons minced chipotle pepper in adobo sauce

2 tablespoons chopped fresh cilantro

1 teaspoon ground cumin

½ teaspoon lime zest

2 teaspoons fresh lime juice

3 cups shredded rotisserie chicken

2 tablespoons butter, softened

8 (8-inch) flour tortillas

2 cups (8 ounces) shredded Monterey Jack cheese

Salsa or pico de gallo

1 Preheat the oven to 425°F or your grill to medium-high heat.

2 Combine the ranch dressing, chipotle, cilantro, cumin, lime zest, juice, and chicken in a large bowl, tossing until well blended.

3 Spread the butter evenly on one side of all the tortillas. Place 4 tortillas, buttered side down, in the center of four pieces of foil. Spoon the chicken mixture evenly onto the four tortillas. Top the chicken mixture evenly with the cheese.

4 Place the remaining 4 tortillas on top of the quesadilla, buttered side up. Place the remaining four pieces of foil flat on top.

5 Fold the foil over the mixture and crimp the edges for flat packages. Cook for 5 minutes; turn over and cook for 3 to 5 additional minutes, until hot and melted. Serve with salsa or pico de gallo.

THAI CHICKEN BURGERS

2 tablespoons soy sauce

1 teaspoon lime zest

1 tablespoon fresh lime juice

1 tablespoon light brown sugar

2 teaspoons chili-garlic paste or sriracha sauce

2 teaspoons sesame oil (optional)

1 pound lean ground chicken or turkey

1 red bell pepper, chopped

2 carrots, shredded

2 green onions, sliced

¼ cup chopped fresh cilantro

2 tablespoons chopped fresh mint

8 bibb or green lettuce leaves

Sweetened chili sauce (optional)

Ground chicken is mild-flavored and very lean, making it a good choice for using as a base for this unique burger.

×

OVEN TEMPERATURE 375°F   **GRILL** MEDIUM HEAT
FOIL 4 SHEETS NONSTICK FOIL OR
FOIL LIGHTLY COATED WITH COOKING SPRAY
SIZE 12" X 15"   **FLAT** PACKAGE   **SERVES** 4

×

1 Preheat the oven to 375°F or your grill to medium heat.

2 Combine the soy sauce, lime zest, lime juice, brown sugar, chili-garlic paste, and sesame oil, if using, in a large bowl, stirring until well blended. Add the ground chicken, bell pepper, carrots, green onions, cilantro, and mint, mixing well.

3 Form the chicken mixture into four patties. Place one patty in the center of each piece of foil.

4 Fold the foil over the burger and crimp the edges for flat packages. Cook for 10 minutes; turn over and cook for an additional 15 minutes, until the chicken is cooked through.

5 Remove from the foil and serve the patties in lettuce leaves. Drizzle with chili sauce, if desired.

THANKSGIVING SAMMIES

1 tablespoon butter, softened

½ teaspoon poultry seasoning
   or ground sage

4 slices potato bread or walnut
   bread with cranberries

¼ cup whole-berry cranberry
   sauce

½ cup baby spinach or arugula

4 ounces sliced roasted
   or smoked deli turkey

2 thin slices baby Swiss cheese

¼ cup packaged fried onions

All of the best flavors of Thanksgiving are layered in this yummy sandwich.

—————— ✕ ——————

OVEN TEMPERATURE 375°F   **GRILL** MEDIUM HEAT
FOIL 2 SHEETS NONSTICK FOIL OR
FOIL LIGHTLY COATED WITH COOKING SPRAY
SIZE 12" X 12"   **FLAT** PACKAGE   **SERVES** 2

—————— ✕ ——————

1 Preheat the oven to 375°F or your grill to medium heat.

2 Combine the butter and poultry seasoning in a small bowl; spread the butter mixture on one side of each piece of bread. Spread the cranberry sauce evenly over the butter.

3 Layer the spinach, turkey, cheese, and fried onions evenly over the cranberry sauce. Top with the remaining two slices of bread, butter and cranberry side down.

4 Fold the foil over the mixture and crimp the edges for flat packages. Cook for 20 minutes, until the sandwiches are hot and the cheese is melted.

BEEF FAJITAS

2 tablespoons extra-virgin olive oil

1 tablespoon ground cumin

1 tablespoon chili powder

1 teaspoon fine sea salt

½ teaspoon smoked paprika

½ teaspoon garlic powder

1 pound top sirloin, skirt steak, or beef tenderloin, sliced into ¼-inch strips

1 small green bell pepper, cut into strips

1 red, yellow, or orange bell pepper, cut into strips

1 small onion, thinly sliced

8 flour or corn tortillas

1 lime, cut into wedges

¼ cup lightly packed fresh cilantro

Sour cream

Salsa

Ground paprika comes in a few varieties—sweet, hot, or smoked. It's made by drying and grinding red peppers. Sweet paprika, sometimes just labeled as "paprika," is made from sweet red peppers. Hot comes from spicy peppers. The peppers used for smoked paprika can be either sweet or hot, so taste a bit of the jar to prevent over-seasoning.

×

OVEN TEMPERATURE 375°F   **GRILL** MEDIUM HEAT

FOIL 5 SHEETS NONSTICK FOIL OR FOIL LIGHTLY COATED WITH COOKING SPRAY

SIZE 12" X 15"   **TENT-STYLE** PACKAGE (FAJITAS)

FLAT PACKAGE (TORTILLAS)   **SERVES** 4

×
---

1 Preheat the oven to 375°F or your grill to medium heat.

2 Combine the oil, cumin, chili powder, salt, smoked paprika, and garlic powder in a large bowl. Add the beef, bell peppers, and onion, tossing to coat. Spoon the fajita mixture evenly into the center of each piece of foil.

3 Fold the foil over the beef mixture and crimp the edges for tent-style packages. Cook for 25 minutes, until the beef is cooked through.

4 Wrap the tortillas in foil and cook for 5 minutes, until hot.

5 Transfer the fajita mixture to the tortillas. Squeeze the lime wedges over. Top evenly with the cilantro and dollop with your desired amount of sour cream and salsa.

PHILLY CHEESESTEAK SANDWICHES

½ sweet onion, sliced

1 green bell pepper, thinly sliced

1 tablespoon extra-virgin olive oil

1 tablespoon Italian seasoning

1 teaspoon beef bouillon granules

¼ teaspoon freshly ground black pepper

¼ teaspoon garlic powder

1½ pounds lean rib eye, sirloin, or other beef steak

4 slices provolone cheese

4 hoagie rolls, split

It's all about the beef! Select a high-flavor meat like a rib eye. Instead of salt, sprinkle with beef bouillon granules.

— ✕ —

OVEN TEMPERATURE 375°F **GRILL** MEDIUM HEAT
FOIL 4 SHEETS HEAVY-DUTY NONSTICK FOIL OR FOIL LIGHTLY COATED WITH COOKING SPRAY
SIZE 12" X 18" **TENT-STYLE** PACKAGE **SERVES** 4

— ✕ —

1 Preheat the oven to 375°F or your grill to medium heat.

2 Combine the onion, bell pepper, oil, seasoning, bouillon, pepper, and garlic powder in a large bowl, stirring until the vegetables are coated. Divide the vegetables evenly and place in the center of each piece of foil.

3 Trim the fat away from the beef. Slice the meat into very thin strips and place evenly over the vegetables.

4 Fold the foil over the beef and crimp the edges for tent-style packages. Cook for 20 to 25 minutes, until the meat is done and the vegetables are tender.

5 Carefully open the foil and top each bundle with a slice of cheese. Fold the foil together and let the packages stand for 1 minute, until the cheese melts. Spoon the mixture evenly into the rolls.

INSIDE-OUT PIMIENTO CHEESE-BURGERS

1 cup (4 ounces) shredded sharp cheddar cheese

1 tablespoon mayonnaise

1 teaspoon Worcestershire sauce

¼ teaspoon hot sauce

¼ teaspoon freshly ground black pepper

1 tablespoon chopped pimientos or roasted red bell pepper

1½ pounds very lean ground beef

4 buns

Optional toppings: lettuce, tomato, pickled jalapeños, ketchup

These cheese-stuffed burgers are juicy! Press the edges carefully so they don't "unstuff" while cooking. Chilling the burgers for at least 30 minutes helps, as well as cooking them quickly over high heat.

— ✕ —

OVEN TEMPERATURE 375°F **GRILL** MEDIUM HEAT
FOIL 4 SHEETS HEAVY-DUTY NONSTICK FOIL OR FOIL LIGHTLY COATED WITH COOKING SPRAY
SIZE 12" X 18" **FLAT** PACKAGE **SERVES** 4

— ✕ —

1 Preheat the oven to 375°F or your grill to medium heat.

2 Combine the cheese, mayonnaise, Worcestershire, hot sauce, pepper, and pimientos in a small bowl.

3 Form the beef into 8 thin patties. Divide the cheese mixture evenly on top of 4 patties. Top with the remaining 4 patties and press around the burger to seal the edges completely. Cover and chill for 30 minutes or overnight.

4 Place a patty in the center of each piece of foil. Fold the foil over the patties and crimp the edges for flat packages.

5 Cook for 15 minutes. Turn the packages over and cook for an additional 10 minutes. Serve between the buns, with your desired toppings.

TOASTED MUFFULETTA SANDWICHES

This New Orleans specialty is often served chilled, but is even better heated with slightly melted cheese. Wrap tightly to hold all the ingredients in place.

×

OVEN TEMPERATURE 375°F **GRILL** MEDIUM HEAT

FOIL 2 SHEETS NONSTICK FOIL OR
FOIL LIGHTLY COATED WITH COOKING SPRAY

SIZE 12" X 24" **FLAT** PACKAGE **SERVES** 6

×

OLIVE SALAD

½ cup green olives with pimientos

½ cup pitted black olives

½ cup giardiniera (Italian pickled vegetables)

2 tablespoons extra-virgin olive oil

1 tablespoon capers, drained

1 tablespoon red wine vinegar

2 small garlic cloves, minced

1 (24-ounce) round Italian bread loaf (about 8 inches)

3 tablespoons Creole mustard

⅛ pound sliced ham

⅓ pound sliced roasted or smoked turkey

¼ pound sliced salami

4 slices provolone cheese

4 slices mozzarella or Muenster cheese

1 Preheat the oven to 375°F or your grill to medium heat.

2 First make the Olive Salad: Combine the olives, giardiniera, oil, capers, vinegar, and garlic in a food processor. Pulse until coarsely chopped.

3 Split the bread in half to create a top and bottom. Scoop out about 1½ inches of the bread on each side. (Save the pieces of bread for breadcrumbs.) Spread the mustard in the bottom half. Layer the ham, turkey, and salami over the mustard. Layer the cheeses over the meats.

4 Spread the olive salad evenly over the cheese and top with the bread. Place in the center of one piece of foil. Place the second piece of foil perpendicular to the first piece to completely cover.

5 Fold the foil over the sandwich and crimp the edges for a flat package. Cook for 15 minutes, until thoroughly heated. Cut into 6 wedges to serve.

BLUE CHEESE AND ONION BURGERS

1 tablespoon butter

1 large onion, halved and thinly sliced

1 pound extra-lean ground beef

1 tablespoon Worcestershire sauce

1 teaspoon hot sauce

½ teaspoon fine sea salt

¼ teaspoon freshly ground black pepper

½ cup (2 ounces) crumbled blue cheese

4 brioche or other burger buns, split

4 lettuce leaves

4 slices tomato

Caramelized onions add an amazing flavor to burgers. Making them is time-consuming, but very easy. Stir the onions periodically for the first 15 minutes, then more frequently as they caramelize to avoid scorching.

OVEN TEMPERATURE 375°F **GRILL** MEDIUM HEAT
FOIL 4 SHEETS HEAVY-DUTY NONSTICK FOIL OR FOIL LIGHTLY COATED WITH COOKING SPRAY
SIZE 12" X 18" **FLAT** PACKAGE **SERVES** 4

---

1 Melt the butter in a large heavy skillet over medium heat. Add the onion and cook, stirring frequently, for about 30 minutes, until golden brown and tender. Set aside.

2 Preheat the oven to 375°F or heat your grill to medium heat.

3 Combine the beef, Worcestershire, hot sauce, salt, and pepper in a large bowl. Add the blue cheese, gently folding until evenly blended.

4 Form the beef mixture into 4 patties and place in the center of each piece of foil. Top evenly with the onions. Fold the foil over the mixture and crimp the edges for flat packages.

5 Cook for 15 minutes. Turn the packages over and cook for an additional 10 minutes. Serve with the lettuce and tomato between the buns.

PEPPERONI CHEESE BREAD

This buttery, cheesy, and spicy treat is addictive—you'll find yourself pulling off another piece and saying, "Just one more!" Use nonstick foil, or make sure that all the edges are lightly greased so the cheese doesn't stick. Level up this crowd-pleasing snack by dipping pieces in warm marinara or pasta sauce.

1 (14- to 16-ounce) round or oval bread loaf

½ cup (1 stick) butter, melted

1 tablespoon Italian seasoning

½ teaspoon garlic powder

½ (6-ounce) package sliced pepperoni

1 (8-ounce) package mozzarella cheese, shredded

⅓ cup shredded Parmesan cheese

Marinara sauce (optional)

OVEN TEMPERATURE 350°F   **GRILL** MEDIUM HEAT

FOIL 1 SHEET HEAVY-DUTY NONSTICK FOIL OR FOIL LIGHTLY COATED WITH COOKING SPRAY

SIZE 12" X 24"   **TENT-STYLE** PACKAGE   **SERVES** 6 TO 8

---

1 Preheat the oven to 350°F or your grill to medium heat.

2 Cut the bread into 1½-inch slices almost to the bottom of the loaf. Turn the loaf and make 1½-inch slices to create a crosshatch pattern.

3 Combine the butter, seasoning, and garlic powder in a small bowl. Drizzle or brush the butter mixture into the cuts. Stuff the cuts with the pepperoni and shredded cheeses, letting some of the cheese remain on top.

4 Fold the foil over the mixture and crimp the edges for a tent-style package. Cook for 25 minutes until heated through and the cheese is melted. Tear off pieces and dip in the marinara sauce, if desired.

CRAB CAKES

2 egg whites, slightly beaten

⅔ cup panko or cracker crumbs (about 15 crackers)

2 tablespoons minced green onions

2 tablespoons mayonnaise

½ teaspoon lemon zest

1 tablespoon fresh lemon juice

2 teaspoons chopped fresh parsley

2 teaspoons seafood seasoning

2 teaspoons Dijon mustard

2 teaspoons Worcestershire sauce

1 pound lump crabmeat, picked

6 buns

6 lettuce leaves

6 tomato slices

Prepared tartar or remoulade sauce

This recipe is definitely a keeper, with just the right amount of seasoning to highlight the tender crabmeat. Lump (and especially jumbo lump) crab is expensive. If you want to substitute less expensive backfin, make sure it is drained and picked through very well since it tends to have more tiny bits of shell than either type of lump crab.

OVEN TEMPERATURE 350°F   **GRILL** MEDIUM HEAT
FOIL 6 SHEETS HEAVY-DUTY NONSTICK FOIL OR FOIL LIGHTLY COATED WITH COOKING SPRAY
SIZE 12" X 12"   **FLAT** PACKAGE   **SERVES** 6

---

1 Preheat the oven to 350°F or your grill to medium heat.

2 Combine the egg whites, panko, green onions, mayonnaise, lemon zest, lemon juice, parsley, seasoning, mustard, and Worcestershire in a large bowl. Add the crab, folding gently until well blended.

3 Form the crab mixture into 6 crab cakes, about ½ cup each. Place 1 crab cake on each piece of foil.

4 Fold the foil over the crab cakes and crimp the edges for flat packages. Cook for 15 minutes; turn the packages over and cook for 10 more minutes until the crab cake is firm and cooked through. Serve on buns with lettuce, tomato, and tartar or remoulade sauce.

HAM, BRIE, APPLE, AND ARUGULA CROISSANT SANDWICHES

⅓ cup apricot preserves
or orange marmalade

4 (2- to 2½-ounce) large
croissants, split

1 cup loosely packed cup
baby arugula leaves

8 ounces Brie cheese
(with or without rind),
thinly sliced

1 green or red apple,
cored and thinly sliced

12 ounces spiral-sliced ham
or other deli ham

For the best flavor and texture, use slices from a whole cut ham that is simply a smoked, seasoned piece of meat. These thicker cuts are less pliable than the more common processed ham slices, so you may need to break them into pieces that will fit within the croissant.

—————————— ✕ ——————————

OVEN TEMPERATURE 350°F   **GRILL** MEDIUM HEAT
FOIL 4 SHEETS NONSTICK FOIL OR
FOIL LIGHTLY COATED WITH COOKING SPRAY
SIZE 12" X 12"   **FLAT** PACKAGE   **SERVES** 4

—————————— ✕ ——————————

1 Preheat the oven to 350°F or your grill to medium heat.

2 Spread the preserves on the cut sides of the croissants. On the bottom half, layer the arugula, cheese, apple slices, and ham. Add the top half and place a sandwich in the center of each piece of foil.

3 Fold the foil over the sandwiches and crimp the edges for flat packages. Cook for 15 to 20 minutes, until warm and the cheese is melted.

EGGS FLORENTINE BREAKFAST SANDWICHES

4 large crusty rolls

2 tablespoons melted butter

⅛ teaspoon garlic powder

4 button mushrooms, sliced

4 cherry tomatoes, halved

2 slices bacon, cooked and crumbled

¾ cup baby spinach

4 large eggs

½ teaspoon fine sea salt

¼ teaspoon freshly ground pepper

½ cup (2 ounces) shredded cheddar cheese

Take care to keep the rolls upright when placing in the oven or on the grill so the egg doesn't run out and down the sides. If you prefer scrambled eggs, lightly beat the egg with the salt and pepper and then stir in the cheese. Pour the mixture over the filling.

OVEN TEMPERATURE 350°F   **GRILL** MEDIUM HEAT
FOIL 4 SHEETS NONSTICK FOIL OR
FOIL LIGHTLY COATED WITH COOKING SPRAY
SIZE 12" X 18"   **TENT-STYLE** PACKAGE   **SERVES** 4

---

1 Preheat the oven to 350°F or your grill to medium heat.

2 Slice ¼ inch off the top of each roll. Scoop out the bread to create a ½-inch shell. Save the top and inside of the roll for breadcrumbs. Brush the inside of each roll with butter and sprinkle evenly with garlic powder.

3 Layer the mushrooms, tomatoes, bacon, and spinach evenly in each bread shell. Spread the filling apart to create a hollow space. Crack one egg in the middle of each roll. Sprinkle with the salt, pepper, and shredded cheese.

4 Fold the foil over the mixture and crimp the edges for tent-style packages. Cook for 35 minutes, until cooked through.

FISH TACOS WITH CHIPOTLE-LIME CREMA

1½ pounds boneless, skinless Pacific halibut

1 tablespoon extra-virgin olive oil

1 tablespoon ancho chili powder

1 tablespoon ground cumin

½ teaspoon garlic powder

1 teaspoon fine sea salt

½ teaspoon freshly ground black pepper

8 (5-inch) corn tortillas

½ cup finely shredded cabbage

¼ cup chopped fresh cilantro

Salsa or pico de gallo

CHIPOTLE-LIME CREMA
½ cup sour cream

1 chipotle pepper in adobo sauce, minced

1 tablespoon adobo sauce

½ teaspoon lime zest

1 tablespoon fresh lime juice

¼ teaspoon fine sea salt

Flatfish or thin fillets often break apart when grilled directly over the heat. Wrapping the tender fish in foil keeps the pieces intact and out of the coals. I suggest Pacific halibut here, but cod, tilapia, or any other mild whitefish would do.

✕

OVEN TEMPERATURE 375°F   **GRILL** MEDIUM HEAT
FOIL 5 SHEETS NONSTICK FOIL OR FOIL LIGHTLY COATED WITH COOKING SPRAY
SIZE 12" X 15"   **TENT-STYLE** PACKAGE (FISH)
FLAT PACKAGE (TORTILLAS)   **SERVES** 4

✕
---

1 Preheat the oven to 375°F or your grill to medium heat.

2 Cut the fish into 4 equal portions. Place each piece of fish in the center of a piece of foil. Brush the fish evenly with the oil and sprinkle evenly with the chili powder, cumin, garlic powder, salt, and pepper.

3 Fold the foil over the mixture and crimp the edges for tent-style packages. Wrap the tortillas in the remaining piece of foil and crimp edges for a flat package.

4 Cook the fish for 20 minutes, until the fish is cooked through. About 5 minutes before the fish is done, place the wrapped tortillas on the grill or in the oven and cook until heated through.

5 Meanwhile, make the Chipotle-Lime Crema: Combine the sour cream, chipotle pepper, adobo sauce, lime zest, lime juice, and salt in a small bowl.

6 Break the cooked fish into pieces and place on the warm tortillas. Top with the cabbage, cilantro, salsa, and Chipotle-Lime Crema.

GREEK-STYLE TUNA MELT IN PITA BREAD

2 (6-ounce) cans water- or oil-packed tuna, well drained

3 small celery stalks, minced

½ teaspoon lemon zest

1 tablespoon fresh lemon juice

¼ cup mayonnaise

12 pitted Kalamata olives, chopped

2 teaspoons chopped fresh oregano

½ teaspoon freshly ground black pepper

2 whole (6- to 8-inch) pitas or 4 (4- to 6-inch) pitas or flatbreads

¼ red onion, thinly sliced

6 thin slices Muenster or smoked provolone cheese

¼ seedless hothouse cucumber, thinly sliced

1 tomato, thinly sliced and seeded

1 tablespoon butter, softened

One thing to watch out for when using tomatoes is too much liquid. To keep these zesty sandwiches from getting soggy, place the tomato slices on paper towels and pick away the seeds. If you can't find seedless cucumbers, split a regular cucumber in half lengthwise and scoop out the seeds before slicing. Some pita bread is hollow in the center and can be cut in half to create pockets. Some smaller versions are thick throughout. Cut those in half and layer the ingredients as you would for a traditional sandwich.

OVEN TEMPERATURE 375°F   **GRILL** MEDIUM HEAT
FOIL 4 SHEETS NONSTICK FOIL OR FOIL LIGHTLY COATED WITH COOKING SPRAY
SIZE 12" X 18"   **FLAT** PACKAGE   **SERVES** 4

---

1 Preheat the oven to 375°F or your grill to medium heat.

2 Combine the tuna, celery, lemon zest, lemon juice, mayonnaise, olives, oregano, and pepper in a bowl.

3 Cut the pitas in half and open, if possible, to create pockets. Divide the onion, cheese, cucumber, and tomato evenly and place inside the pitas. Spoon the tuna evenly into the pockets.

4 Spread the butter lightly on the outside of the pitas and place a pita in the center of each piece of foil. Fold the foil over and crimp the edges for flat packages.

5 Cook for 5 minutes; turn over and cook an additional 3 to 5 minutes, until warmed through and the cheese is melted.

SALMON BURGERS

2 large eggs

½ cup Greek yogurt

¼ cup roasted red bell pepper, finely chopped

2 tablespoons minced red onion

½ teaspoon lemon zest

1 tablespoon fresh lemon juice

2 teaspoons capers, drained well

2 teaspoons Dijon mustard

½ teaspoon fine sea salt

¼ teaspoon freshly ground black pepper

¼ teaspoon fresh or dried dill

1 (14.75-ounce) can wild salmon, drained and flaked

¾ cup seasoned or plain panko breadcrumbs

4 buns

4 lettuce leaves

4 tomato slices

QUICK TZAZIKI SAUCE

½ cup plain Greek yogurt

1 minced garlic clove

¼ cup minced cucumber

1 teaspoon chopped fresh dill

¼ teaspoon salt

Canned salmon is a great way to reap all the health benefits of wild salmon at a fraction of the cost. It may be disconcerting to see skin and some bones inside the can, but don't fret. The canning process makes them completely edible. You'll see the bones disintegrate when stirred, and they add a good amount of calcium to the dish. If you're bothered by them, you can remove the skin and bone pieces. Pink salmon is most commonly used for canned. Sockeye is occasionally canned but is about double the cost.

✕

OVEN TEMPERATURE 375°F   **GRILL** MEDIUM HEAT
FOIL 4 SHEETS HEAVY-DUTY NONSTICK FOIL OR FOIL LIGHTLY COATED WITH COOKING SPRAY
SIZE 12" X 15"   **FLAT** PACKAGE   **SERVES** 4

✕

1 Preheat the oven to 375°F or your grill to medium heat.

2 Whisk the eggs in a large bowl. Stir in the yogurt, bell pepper, onion, lemon zest, lemon juice, capers, mustard, salt, pepper, and dill. Fold in the salmon and breadcrumbs with a spatula, stirring until well blended.

3 Divide into 4 equal portions, place in the center of each piece of foil, and shape into patties.

4 Fold the foil over the salmon patties and crimp the edges to seal into a flat package. Refrigerate, up to a day ahead, until ready to cook.

5 Before you are ready to cook the salmon patties, make the Quick Tzaziki Sauce: Combine the yogurt, garlic, cucumber, dill, and salt in a medium bowl.

6 Cook the salmon burgers for 5 minutes; turn over and cook for 5 additional minutes. Dollop the Quick Tzaziki Sauce over the burgers and serve between the buns with lettuce and tomato.

CHAPTER 5

FROM THE GARDEN

Every meal should include vegetables.

The list of reasons why is long, with an emphasis on health, but that shortchanges the bountiful rainbow. Vegetables taste good! Here, vegetables and vegetarian entrées are grouped together, since one person's veggie side dish is another's light vegetarian dinner. Vegetarians may build their diet on produce, but even omnivores want a little veggie variety. If you want to pump up the protein, add your favorite cooked meat. Leftovers are ideal—toss in a cup of shredded rotisserie or grilled chicken, diced ham, bacon, and so on. Cooked meats are best since they won't require any additional cooking time. If you choose to add raw meat, select lean cuts and increase cooking time to ensure it's completely cooked.

RECURSE LIST

—— × ——

GARLIC-BUTTER BROCCOLINI

2 tablespoons butter, melted

1 garlic clove, minced

⅛ teaspoon crushed red pepper flakes

1 bunch broccolini or broccoli florets (8 ounces), cut into pieces

¼ cup shredded Parmesan cheese

Balsamic glaze (optional)

Balsamic glaze is a condiment found near the oils and vinegars that adds a sweet and zesty flavor to meats, vegetables, and cheeses like fresh mozzarella. Basically, it's sweetened balsamic vinegar that's been cooked down until syrupy. To make your own, simmer 1 cup balsamic vinegar and ¼ cup light brown sugar over medium-low heat, stirring occasionally.

✕

OVEN TEMPERATURE 375°F **GRILL** MEDIUM HEAT
FOIL 4 SHEETS NONSTICK FOIL OR FOIL LIGHTLY COATED WITH COOKING SPRAY
SIZE 12" X 15" **TENT-STYLE** PACKAGE **SERVES** 2

✕

1 Preheat the oven to 375°F or your grill to medium heat.

2 Combine the butter, garlic, and pepper flakes in a large bowl. Add the broccolini and toss until well coated. Add the cheese, tossing until well blended. Divide the broccolini evenly and place in the center of each piece of foil.

3 Fold the foil over the vegetables and crimp the edges for tent-style packages. Cook for 15 minutes, until the vegetables are cooked through. Serve with the balsamic glaze, if desired.

CHEESY-GARLIC SCALLOPED POTATOES

½ cup heavy whipping cream

4 tablespoons butter, melted

¾ teaspoon fine sea salt

¼ teaspoon freshly ground black pepper

2 large garlic cloves, minced

1 pound Yukon gold potatoes, thinly sliced

1 cup (4 ounces) shredded cheddar cheese

⅓ cup freshly grated Parmesan cheese

Potato skins add nutrition and flavor, but you can peel them if you wish. Be sure the potatoes are sliced at the same width, about ⅛ inch thick, so they cook at the same time.

×

OVEN TEMPERATURE 300°F   **GRILL** MEDIUM-LOW HEAT
FOIL 4 SHEETS NONSTICK FOIL OR
FOIL LIGHTLY COATED WITH COOKING SPRAY
SIZE 12" X 18"   **TENT-STYLE** PACKAGE   **SERVES** 2

×

1 Preheat the oven to 300°F or your grill to medium-low heat.

2 Combine the cream, butter, salt, pepper, and garlic in a medium bowl.

3 Place the potatoes and cheese in a large bowl; toss gently to combine. Pour the butter mixture over the potatoes, stirring until well blended. Divide the potato mixture evenly and place in the center of each piece of foil.

4 Fold the foil over the mixture and crimp the edges for tent-style packages. Cook for 40 minutes, until the potatoes are tender.

POTATO-SOY CHORIZO HASH

More and more meat substitutes are available in markets. Often made from soy or tofu-based products, they can be bland on their own, so look for varieties seasoned with a lot of spice. Trader Joe's sells a popular soy chorizo product. It's sticky and sometimes difficult to stir but adds an immense (and delicious) flavor.

— ✕ —

OVEN TEMPERATURE 375°F   **GRILL** MEDIUM HEAT
FOIL 6 SHEETS HEAVY-DUTY NONSTICK FOIL OR FOIL LIGHTLY COATED WITH COOKING SPRAY
SIZE 12" X 18"   **TENT-STYLE** PACKAGE   **SERVES** 6

— ✕ —

2 tablespoons olive oil

1 teaspoon chili powder

1 teaspoon ground cumin

1½ teaspoons fine sea salt

1 large yellow gold or russet potato, cubed

2 medium sweet potatoes, peeled and cubed

1 small onion, chopped

2 cups chopped kale

1 (6- to 8-ounce) package vegetarian soy-based, Mexican-style chorizo or spicy meatless crumbles

1 Preheat the oven to 375°F or your grill to medium heat.

2 Combine the oil, chili powder, cumin, and salt in a large bowl. Add the potatoes, onion, and kale; toss until coated.

3 Remove the chorizo from the casing, if necessary, and break into small pieces. Stir the chorizo into the potato mixture and spoon it evenly into the center of each piece of foil.

4 Fold the foil over the potato mixture and crimp the edges for tent-style packages. Cook for 35 minutes, until the potatoes are cooked.

POTATO-ZUCCHINI BAKE

2 tablespoons extra-virgin olive oil

1 teaspoon chopped fresh rosemary

¾ teaspoon fine sea salt

¼ teaspoon freshly ground black pepper

⅛ teaspoon crushed red pepper flakes

½ pound baby red potatoes, halved

2 zucchini, quartered and sliced

1 large garlic clove, very thinly sliced

Waxy or all-purpose potatoes such as red or fingerlings hold their shape when cooked in soups, stews, or casseroles. Use starchy potatoes with a fluffy texture, like russets, for frying or baking.

—————————— ✕ ——————————

OVEN TEMPERATURE 375°F   **GRILL** MEDIUM HEAT

FOIL 2 SHEETS HEAVY-DUTY FOIL

SIZE 12" X 18"   **TENT-STYLE** PACKAGE   **SERVES** 4

—————————— ✕ ——————————

1 Preheat the oven to 375°F or your grill to medium heat.

2 Combine the oil, rosemary, salt, pepper, and pepper flakes in a large bowl. Add the potatoes, zucchini, and garlic. Stir until the vegetables are coated in oil.

3 Divide the vegetables evenly and spoon into the center of each piece of foil. Fold the foil over the vegetables and crimp the edges for tent-style packages. Cook for 35 minutes, until the potatoes are tender.

SWEET AND SPICY GREEN BEANS

4 tablespoons butter

¼ cup packed light brown sugar

1 tablespoon soy sauce

2 teaspoons Worcestershire sauce

⅛ teaspoon crushed red pepper flakes

12 ounces fresh *haricots verts* or other thin green beans

Hot cooked rice (optional)

This sweet and salty side is perfect for diners preferring the crisp-tender consistency of lightly steamed green beans. If you prefer very soft vegetables, blanch the beans in boiling water for 3 to 5 minutes before assembling. The mixture gets saucy as it cooks—serve over hot cooked rice, or spoon ½ cup cooked rice for each serving onto the foil, then top with the buttered green beans.

OVEN TEMPERATURE 350°F   **GRILL** MEDIUM HEAT

FOIL 6 SHEETS HEAVY-DUTY NONSTICK FOIL OR FOIL LIGHTLY COATED WITH COOKING SPRAY

SIZE 12" X 15"   **TENT-STYLE** PACKAGE   **SERVES** 6

---

1 Preheat the oven to 350°F or your grill to medium heat.

2 Combine the butter, brown sugar, soy sauce, Worcestershire, and pepper flakes in a glass bowl. Microwave on high for 30 seconds, until the butter melts; stir until well blended.

3 Toss the beans in the butter mixture and place evenly in the center of each piece of foil. Fold the foil over the vegetables and crimp the edges for tent-style packages.

4 Cook for 25 minutes, until the beans are tender. Serve over rice, if desired.

HONEY ROASTED ROOT VEGETABLES

MIX AND MATCH, JUST USE ABOUT 2 POUNDS TOTAL

1 sweet potato, peeled and cubed

1 beet, peeled and cubed

2 orange or multicolored carrots, sliced

2 parsnips, peeled and chopped

1 red onion, cut into thin wedges

2 garlic cloves, minced

1 teaspoon chopped fresh rosemary

1 teaspoon fine sea salt

¼ teaspoon freshly ground black pepper

3 tablespoons butter, melted

2 tablespoons local honey

A little bit of honey accentuates the natural sweetness of these sturdy root vegetables. Remember to cut or cube them to the same size so the ingredients cook evenly and all become tender at the same time.

×

OVEN TEMPERATURE 400°F   **GRILL** MEDIUM-HIGH HEAT

FOIL 4 SHEETS HEAVY-DUTY NONSTICK FOIL OR FOIL LIGHTLY COATED WITH COOKING SPRAY

SIZE 12" X 18"   **TENT-STYLE** PACKAGE   **SERVES** 6

×

1 Preheat the oven to 400°F or your grill to medium-high heat.

2 Combine the sweet potato, beet, carrots, parsnips, onion, and garlic in a large bowl. Stir in the rosemary, salt, and pepper.

3 Melt the butter in a small glass container in the microwave and stir in the honey. Add the butter mixture into the vegetables, stirring until well coated.

4 Divide the vegetables evenly and place in the center of each piece of foil. Fold the foil over the mixture and crimp the edges for tent-style packages.

5 If baking in the oven, place the packages on a baking sheet. Cook for 35 minutes, until the vegetables are tender. Halfway through cooking, pick up the top of each package with tongs and give it a little shake to stir the contents.

SIMPLE RATATOUILLE

2 tablespoons extra-virgin olive oil

2 tablespoons tomato paste

2 tablespoons white wine

1 teaspoon dried Italian seasoning

1 teaspoon fine sea salt

¼ teaspoon freshly ground black pepper

⅛ teaspoon crushed red pepper flakes

2 large tomatoes, seeded and diced

2 garlic cloves, minced

1 zucchini, halved and sliced

1 yellow squash, halved and sliced

1 red, yellow, or orange bell pepper, diced

1 small sweet onion, quartered and sliced

2 tablespoons chopped fresh basil

¾ cup shredded Parmesan cheese

This flavorful homage to summer vegetables is hearty enough to serve as a main dish. For an even more filling meal, serve over pasta.

OVEN TEMPERATURE 375°F   **GRILL** MEDIUM HEAT
FOIL 4 SHEETS NONSTICK FOIL OR FOIL LIGHTLY COATED WITH COOKING SPRAY
SIZE 12" X 18"   **TENT-STYLE** PACKAGE   **SERVES** 4

---

1 Preheat the oven to 375°F or your grill to medium heat.

2 Combine the oil, tomato paste, wine, Italian seasoning, salt, pepper, and pepper flakes in a large bowl. Stir in the tomatoes, garlic, zucchini, squash, bell pepper, onion, and basil.

3 Divide the vegetable mixture evenly and place in the center of each piece of foil. Sprinkle each bundle evenly with the Parmesan cheese.

4 Fold the foil over the vegetables and crimp the edges for tent-style packages. Cook for 30 minutes, until the vegetables are hot and tender.

MISO-MAPLE WINTER SQUASH

1 (2½-pound) butternut squash

⅓ cup white, red, or brown miso paste

3 tablespoons maple syrup

1 tablespoon low-sodium soy or tamari sauce

1 tablespoon sesame oil

Cutting butternut squash can be tough—it's dense. To make it easier to slice, microwave the squash on high for 1 to 2 minutes. Let it rest until cool enough to handle, then peel and cut with a good chef's knife.

—————————— ✗ ——————————

OVEN TEMPERATURE 350°F   **GRILL** MEDIUM HEAT
FOIL 4 SHEETS NONSTICK FOIL OR
FOIL LIGHTLY COATED WITH COOKING SPRAY
SIZE 12" X 15"   **TENT-STYLE** PACKAGE   **SERVES** 4

—————————— ✗ ——————————

1 Preheat the oven to 350°F or your grill to medium heat.

2 Cut the squash in half and scoop out the seeds. Peel off the skin with a sharp knife or vegetable peeler. Cut the squash into wedges or long pieces about 1 inch wide and 3 inches long.

3 Combine the miso paste, maple syrup, soy sauce, and sesame oil in a large bowl. Toss the squash in the miso mixture. Divide the squash evenly and place in the center of each foil sheet.

4 Fold the foil over the squash and crimp the edges for tent-style packages. Cook for 35 minutes, until the squash is tender.

SPICED ACORN SQUASH RINGS

Unlike many other types of winter squash, the skin on acorn squash is tender enough to eat. Don't worry about peeling!

— ✕ —

OVEN TEMPERATURE 325°F **GRILL** MEDIUM-LOW HEAT
FOIL 2 SHEETS HEAVY-DUTY NONSTICK FOIL OR FOIL LIGHTLY COATED WITH COOKING SPRAY
SIZE 12" X 15" **TENT-STYLE** PACKAGE **SERVES** 2

— ✕ —

2 tablespoons butter, melted

¼ cup firmly packed light brown sugar

1 teaspoon ground cinnamon

¼ teaspoon ground cumin

¼ teaspoon ground coriander

¼ teaspoon fine sea salt

1 large acorn squash

1 Preheat the oven to 325°F or your grill to medium-low heat.

2 Combine the butter, brown sugar, cinnamon, cumin, coriander, and salt in a bowl.

3 Cut the squash into ¼-inch rings and discard the seeds. Spread the squash with the spiced butter mixture and divide the rings evenly in the center of each piece of foil.

4 Fold the foil over the squash and crimp the edges for tent-style packages. Cook for 30 minutes, until tender.

BIG BATCH SUCCOTASH

Buying frozen corn kernels, okra, and lima beans means you can make this year-round. If using, make sure to thaw and drain thoroughly since frozen veggies often release water, diluting the flavor.

OVEN TEMPERATURE 350°F   **GRILL** MEDIUM HEAT
FOIL 6 SHEETS NONSTICK FOIL OR
FOIL LIGHTLY COATED WITH COOKING SPRAY
SIZE 12" X 18"   **TENT-STYLE** PACKAGE   **SERVES** 6

---

4 ears corn or 3 cups corn kernels

1 (10-ounce) package frozen baby lima beans, thawed and drained

2 cups fresh or frozen and thawed okra, sliced

2 cups cherry tomatoes, halved

½ small sweet onion, chopped

1 jalapeño pepper, seeded and minced

2 garlic cloves, minced

3 tablespoons butter, melted

2 tablespoons apple cider vinegar

2 tablespoons chopped fresh chives

2 tablespoons chopped fresh basil

1 tablespoon fresh thyme leaves

½ teaspoon smoked paprika

1½ teaspoons fine sea salt

½ teaspoon freshly ground black pepper

1 Preheat the oven to 350°F or your grill to medium heat.

2 Cut the kernels from the corn and place in a large bowl. Stir in the lima beans, okra, tomatoes, onion, pepper, and garlic. Stir in the butter, vinegar, chives, basil, thyme, paprika, salt, and pepper.

3 Divide the vegetable mixture evenly and place in the center of each piece of foil. Fold the foil over the vegetable mixture and crimp the edges for tent-style packages. Cook for 25 minutes, until the vegetables are hot.

SUMMER SQUASH SPIRALS WITH RICOTTA AND BASIL

Spiralizing vegetables gets trendy every now and again, but it's particularly useful now that low-carb and gluten-free diets need replacements for wheat pasta. Summer squash is my favorite for cutting into those funky long loops because the device naturally removes the center core where the seeds are, making the squash even more tender.

✕

OVEN TEMPERATURE 350°F   **GRILL** MEDIUM HEAT
FOIL 4 SHEETS NONSTICK FOIL OR
FOIL LIGHTLY COATED WITH COOKING SPRAY
SIZE 12" X 18"   **TENT-STYLE** PACKAGE   **SERVES** 4

✕

¾ cup ricotta cheese

½ cup shredded Parmesan cheese

1 garlic clove, minced

¼ cup chopped fresh basil

½ teaspoon fine sea salt

¼ teaspoon freshly ground black pepper

2 zucchini

1 yellow squash

1 Preheat the oven to 350°F or your grill to medium heat.

2 Combine the ricotta, Parmesan, garlic, basil, salt, and pepper in a small bowl. Set aside.

3 Cut the zucchini and yellow squash into long thin ribbons with a spiral cutter. Alternatively, you can slice the squash about ⅛ to ¼ inch thick.

4 Divide the vegetables evenly and place in the center of each foil sheet. Spoon the cheese mixture evenly over the vegetables.

5 Fold the foil over the mixture and crimp the edges for tent-style packages. If baking in the oven, place the packages on a baking sheet in case they leak. If grilling, preheat to medium heat, and reduce to low heat just before putting the packages on the grill rack. Cook for 15 to 20 minutes, until the veggies are tender and the cheese is hot and slightly melted.

CAULIFLOWER WITH ROMESCO SAUCE

Romesco is a classic Spanish sauce made from roasted peppers and tomatoes, with added texture coming from toasted almonds. Nicely paired here with cauliflower, try the sauce over grilled fish or chicken, too.

OVEN TEMPERATURE 375°F   **GRILL** MEDIUM HEAT

FOIL 4 SHEETS NONSTICK FOIL OR FOIL LIGHTLY COATED WITH COOKING SPRAY

SIZE 12" X 15"   **TENT-STYLE** PACKAGE   **SERVES** 4

---

1 large ripe tomato, quartered and seeded

2 jarred or fresh roasted red bell peppers, seeded and drained

1 tablespoon sherry vinegar

⅛ teaspoon crushed red pepper flakes

1 tablespoon extra-virgin olive oil

3 tablespoons toasted slivered almonds

1 garlic clove, minced

1 teaspoon fine sea salt

1 teaspoon smoked paprika

4 cups cauliflower florets

3 green onions, cut into 1-inch pieces

1 Preheat the oven to 375°F or your grill to medium heat.

2 Combine the tomato, bell peppers, vinegar, red pepper flakes, oil, almonds, garlic, salt, and paprika in the container of a blender. Blend on low speed for 1 minute; blend on high speed until smooth.

3 Divide the cauliflower and green onions evenly and place in the center of each piece of foil. Spoon the sauce evenly over the vegetables.

4 Fold the foil over the vegetables and crimp the edges for tent-style packages. Cook for 30 minutes, until the vegetables are tender and hot.

CHEESY RICED CAULIFLOWER

1 small head cauliflower
   (2 pounds) or 3 cups riced
   cauliflower

2 large egg whites

2 garlic cloves, minced

2 tablespoons chopped fresh
   basil or flat-leaf parsley

1 teaspoon fine sea salt

½ teaspoon freshly ground
   black pepper

½ cup shredded cheddar
   cheese

½ cup shredded Parmesan
   cheese

3 green onions, sliced

"Riced" cauliflower gained popularity when dieters found it could be a yummy substitution for carb-heavy rice. While this recipe is keto-friendly, it's also too delicious not to be a part of any dinner.

OVEN TEMPERATURE 375°F   **GRILL** MEDIUM HEAT

FOIL 4 SHEETS NONSTICK FOIL OR
FOIL LIGHTLY COATED WITH COOKING SPRAY

SIZE 12" X 18"   **FLAT** PACKAGE   **SERVES** 4

---

1 Preheat the oven to 375°F or your grill to medium heat.

2 Remove the core from the cauliflower and cut into small florets. Place the cauliflower in a food processor. Pulse several times, scraping down the sides with a spatula, until the cauliflower resembles rice.

3 Combine the eggs, garlic, basil, salt, and pepper in a large bowl. Stir in the cauliflower, cheddar, and Parmesan.

4 Divide the cauliflower mixture evenly and place in the center of each piece of foil. Pat the cauliflower patty into a rectangle. Sprinkle evenly with the green onions.

5 Fold the foil over the mixture and crimp the edges for flat packages. Cook for 15 minutes, until hot and cooked through.

MEXICAN STREET CORN

2 tablespoons mayonnaise

1 teaspoon grated lime zest

1 teaspoon fresh lime juice

1 small jalapeño, seeded and minced

1 teaspoon fine sea salt

½ teaspoon chili powder

¼ teaspoon smoked paprika

4 ears fresh corn

1 small red bell pepper, diced

½ cup grated Cotija or Parmesan cheese

¼ cup chopped fresh cilantro

In Mexican food stalls, grilled corn on the cob is spread with a creamy sauce, seasoned with chili pepper and lime, and then sprinkled with a crumbly cheese. This version combines the steps into a simple foil pouch, making it easier and less messy to eat. For a smokier flavor, grill the ears of fresh corn just until lightly charred before cutting off the cob.

✕

OVEN TEMPERATURE 375°F **GRILL** MEDIUM HEAT
FOIL 4 SHEETS HEAVY-DUTY NONSTICK FOIL OR FOIL LIGHTLY COATED WITH COOKING SPRAY
SIZE 12" X 15" **TENT-STYLE** PACKAGE **SERVES** 4

✕

1 Preheat the oven to 375°F or your grill to medium heat.

2 Combine the mayonnaise, lime zest, lime juice, jalapeño, salt, chili powder, and paprika in a large bowl.

3 Cut the kernels from the corn and spoon into the bowl, stirring until well blended. Stir in the bell pepper, cheese, and cilantro.

4 Spoon the mixture evenly into the center of each piece of foil. Fold the foil over the vegetables and crimp the edges for tent-style packages.

5 Cook for 25 minutes, until cooked through.

SWISS CHARD WRAPS WITH SEASONED RICE

Dark leafy greens like Swiss chard make a tasty and healthy wrapper for seasoned rice. Remove the thick rib at the bottom and blanch to make them pliable. Use ruby or saffron-colored types for a pretty package.

OVEN TEMPERATURE 350°F **GRILL** MEDIUM HEAT
FOIL 4 SHEETS NONSTICK FOIL OR FOIL LIGHTLY COATED WITH COOKING SPRAY
SIZE 12" X 16" **FLAT** PACKAGE **SERVES** 4

---

12 large Swiss chard leaves

1½ cups cooked brown or white rice

¼ cup golden raisins

2 tablespoons chopped toasted almonds or pine nuts

1 shallot, minced

1 teaspoon ground cumin

¾ teaspoon ground cinnamon

1 teaspoon lemon zest

1 tablespoon fresh lemon juice

2 tablespoons olive oil

¾ teaspoon fine sea salt

¼ teaspoon freshly ground black pepper

1 Preheat the oven to 350°F or your grill to medium heat.

2 Remove the stems from the greens, keeping the rest of the leaf intact. Cook for 3 minutes in boiling water until limp. Drain into a colander and rinse the leaves with cold water. Place 8 of the leaves on paper towels to dry.

3 Chop the remaining leaves and place in a large bowl. Add the rice, raisins, almonds, shallot, cumin, cinnamon, lemon zest, lemon juice, oil, salt, and pepper; stir the mixture until well blended.

4 Place 1 leaf on a cutting board and top with about ⅓ cup of the rice filling. Roll up, tucking in the sides of the leaf as you go. Repeat with the remaining leaves and filling.

5 Place 2 stuffed leaves in the center of each piece of foil. Fold the foil over the rolls and crimp the edges for flat packages. Cook for 20 minutes, until hot.

WHITE BEANS, KALE, AND ROSEMARY

2 large garlic cloves, minced

2 tablespoons olive oil

2 tablespoons chopped fresh rosemary

1 teaspoon fine sea salt

¼ teaspoon freshly ground black pepper

¼ teaspoon smoked paprika

⅛ teaspoon crushed red pepper flakes

1 (15.5-ounce) can cannellini, great northern, or other white beans, rinsed and drained

8 cups loosely packed chopped fresh kale

There are many kinds of white beans—cannellini, great northern, navy, or baby limas. Use any one of your favorites in this super simple veggie dish. Bean dishes are often cooked with ham or bacon, but the smoked paprika adds a similar earthy flavor.

OVEN TEMPERATURE 375°F   **GRILL** MEDIUM HEAT

FOIL 4 SHEETS NONSTICK FOIL OR FOIL LIGHTLY COATED WITH COOKING SPRAY

SIZE 12" X 18"   **TENT-STYLE** PACKAGE   **SERVES** 4

---

1 Preheat the oven to 375°F or your grill to medium heat.

2 Stir together the garlic, olive oil, rosemary, salt, pepper, smoked paprika, and pepper flakes in a large bowl. Add the beans and kale, tossing to coat well. Spoon the mixture evenly into the center of each piece of foil.

3 Fold the foil over the vegetables and crimp the edges for tent-style packages. Cook for 20 minutes, until the vegetables are hot and tender.

WILD RICE WITH MUSHROOMS AND PECANS

Wild rice isn't rice but a long-grained grass. It takes a while to cook, so it must be prepared before assembling into the foil packages. For more flavor, cook the wild rice with vegetable broth. This dish has wonderful texture.

OVEN TEMPERATURE 375°F **GRILL** MEDIUM HEAT
FOIL 4 SHEETS HEAVY-DUTY NONSTICK FOIL OR FOIL LIGHTLY COATED WITH COOKING SPRAY
SIZE 12" X 18" **TENT-STYLE** PACKAGE **SERVES** 2

---

1 (8-ounce) package uncooked wild rice, rinsed

1 cup sliced shiitake or cremini mushrooms

½ cup coarsely chopped pecans, toasted

¼ cup dried cranberries or cherries

¼ cup extra-virgin olive oil

2 tablespoons apple cider vinegar

1½ teaspoons orange zest

¼ cup fresh orange juice

1 tablespoon honey

1 teaspoon fine sea salt

¼ teaspoon freshly ground black pepper

3 green onions, sliced

1 Cook the wild rice according to package directions. Drain well.

2 Preheat the oven to 375°F or your grill to medium heat.

3 Combine the cooked rice, mushrooms, pecans, cranberries, oil, vinegar, orange zest, orange juice, honey, salt, and pepper. Spoon the rice mixture evenly into the center of each piece of foil. Sprinkle evenly with the green onions.

4 Fold the foil over the mixture and crimp the edges for tent-style packages. Cook for 20 minutes, until hot and tender.

BLACK BEAN ENCHILADAS

The sauce for these enchiladas is easy and delicious—and you may have everything already in your pantry! Warm the tortillas first so they are pliable and easy to roll up. No worries if they tear. Just arrange them on the foil and cover the split with the cheese.

×

OVEN TEMPERATURE 350°F **GRILL** MEDIUM, INDIRECT HEAT (PAGE 4)
FOIL 5 SHEETS HEAVY-DUTY NONSTICK FOIL OR FOIL LIGHTLY COATED WITH COOKING SPRAY
SIZE 12" X 18" **FLAT** PACKAGE (TORTILLAS)
TENT-STYLE PACKAGE (ENCHILADAS) **SERVES** 4

×

QUICK ENCHILADA SAUCE

1 cup vegetable broth

1 tablespoon extra-virgin olive oil

1 tablespoon all-purpose flour

1 tablespoon chili powder

1 tablespoon tomato paste

1 tablespoon apple cider vinegar

2 teaspoons ground cumin

1 teaspoon chipotle peppers in adobo sauce, minced (optional)

¼ teaspoon garlic powder

¼ teaspoon fine sea salt

8 (5-inch) corn tortillas

1 (15.5-ounce) can black beans, rinsed and drained

1 (4-ounce) can diced green chilies

1 red bell pepper, chopped

3 green onions, sliced

2 tablespoons chopped fresh cilantro

1 cup grated Monterey Jack cheese

1 Preheat the oven to 350°F or your grill to medium heat.

2 Prepare the Quick Enchilada Sauce: Whisk together all of the ingredients in a small saucepan over medium-low heat. Simmer for 5 minutes, stirring occasionally, until mixture thickens.

3 Meanwhile, wrap the tortillas in a piece of foil and crimp the edges for a flat package. Cook for 5 minutes, until warm and pliable.

4 Combine the black beans, chilies, bell pepper, green onions, and cilantro in a large bowl. Stir in half of the cheese. Stir in ¼ cup of the enchilada sauce.

5 Spoon 1 tablespoon of the enchilada sauce into the center of each piece of foil.

6 Spoon the black bean mixture evenly onto the tortillas. Roll and place 2 enchiladas, seam side down, on each piece of foil over the sauce. Drizzle the tops evenly with an additional tablespoon of the sauce for each pair of enchiladas. Sprinkle each pair evenly with the remaining cheese.

7 Fold the foil over the mixture and crimp the edges for tent-style packages. If baking in the oven, place the packages on a baking sheet to avoid any spills. If grilling, reduce to low heat just before putting the packages on the grill rack. Cook for 15 to 20 minutes, until hot.

ORANGE BROCCOLI AND SMOKED TOFU

1 navel orange

¼ cup orange marmalade

1 tablespoon soy sauce

2 teaspoons sesame oil

1 teaspoon chili garlic paste
or sriracha

½ teaspoon fine sea salt

3 cups small broccoli florets

¼ cup roasted cashews

1 (7- or 8-ounce) package
smoked or teriyaki-baked
tofu, cubed

Look for smoked or baked tofu in the refrigerated section of grocery stories. Both are dense and firm, and they add more flavor than plain tofu, which will release water when cooked. If you substitute regular tofu, press the blocks between two plates weighted down to remove as much liquid as possible.

✕

OVEN TEMPERATURE 350°F   **GRILL** MEDIUM HEAT
FOIL 4 SHEETS HEAVY-DUTY NONSTICK FOIL OR
FOIL LIGHTLY COATED WITH COOKING SPRAY
SIZE 12" X 15"   **TENT-STYLE** PACKAGE   **SERVES** 2

✕

1 Preheat the oven to 350°F or your grill to medium heat.

2 Grate the orange peel into a large bowl. Peel the orange and cut into segments; set aside.

3 Combine the marmalade, soy sauce, sesame oil, chili paste, and salt in a large bowl. Add the broccoli, cashews, and tofu. Stir lightly until well blended. Add the orange segments, folding gently to avoid breaking them apart.

4 Divide the broccoli mixture evenly and place in the center of each piece of foil. Fold the foil over and crimp the edges for tent-style packages. Cook for 20 minutes, until hot.

QUINOA AND KALE HOT BOWL WITH TAHINI DRESSING

3 cups spiralized butternut squash or carrots (about 6 ounces)

2 cups cooked quinoa

1 (15.5-ounce) can garbanzo beans, rinsed and drained

2 cups lightly packed chopped kale

3 tablespoons extra-virgin olive oil

1 tablespoon apple cider vinegar

1 shallot, minced

1 teaspoon fine sea salt

¼ teaspoon freshly ground black pepper

⅓ cup toasted chopped pumpkin seeds

TAHINI DRESSING

⅓ cup tahini

2 tablespoons fresh lemon juice

2 tablespoons water

1 tablespoon honey

1 garlic clove, minced

¼ teaspoon salt

You can find spiralized butternut squash in grocery stores that offer a lot of value-added services like meal prep, cooked meals, or in-store restaurants. If you have a spiralizer, use the thick upper neck of the butternut and cut up the "bowl" of the squash for other uses.

✕

OVEN TEMPERATURE 375°F   **GRILL** MEDIUM HEAT
FOIL 4 SHEETS HEAVY-DUTY NONSTICK FOIL OR FOIL LIGHTLY COATED WITH COOKING SPRAY
SIZE 12" X 18"   **TENT-STYLE** PACKAGE   **SERVES** 4

✕

1 Preheat the oven to 375°F or your grill to medium heat.

2 Divide the squash evenly and place in the center of each piece of foil. Combine the quinoa, garbanzo beans, and kale in a large bowl. Stir in the olive oil, vinegar, shallot, salt, and pepper. Spoon the mixture evenly over the squash. Sprinkle evenly with the pumpkin seeds.

3 Fold the foil over the mixture and crimp the edges for tent-style packages. Cook for 20 minutes, until the vegetables are hot and tender.

4 Meanwhile, make the Tahini Dressing: Whisk together the tahini, lemon juice, water, honey, garlic, and salt in a small bowl. Serve with the vegetable mixture.

CHEESE TORTELLINI AND ZUCCHINI STEW

1 tablespoon olive oil

¼ medium red onion, chopped

1 garlic clove, minced

1 teaspoon dried Italian seasoning

Pinch of red pepper flakes

½ teaspoon fine sea salt

¼ teaspoon freshly ground black pepper

1 vegetable bouillon cube

1 (14.5-ounce) can basil- or garlic-seasoned diced tomatoes, undrained

1 small zucchini or yellow squash, halved and sliced ¼-inch thick

1 (9-ounce) package refrigerated mixed-cheese tortellini

2 cups chopped kale or spinach

½ cup shredded Parmesan cheese

1 tablespoon chopped fresh basil

The liquid that cooks out of the zucchini and kale to blend with the bouillon cube will be enough to create a light broth for this simple but tasty recipe.

OVEN TEMPERATURE 325°F   **GRILL** MEDIUM-LOW HEAT
FOIL 4 SHEETS NONSTICK FOIL OR FOIL LIGHTLY COATED WITH COOKING SPRAY
SIZE 12" X 18"   **TENT** PACKAGE   **SERVES** 4

---

1 Preheat the oven to 325°F or your grill to medium-low heat.

2 Combine the olive oil, onion, garlic, Italian seasoning, pepper flakes, salt, and pepper in a large bowl. Crush the bouillon cube and stir into the oil mixture.

3 Stir in the tomatoes, zucchini, tortellini, kale, Parmesan, and basil. Spoon the mixture evenly into the center of each piece of foil.

4 Fold the foil over and crimp the edges to form tent-style packages. Cook for 20 minutes, until hot and cooked through.

CHEESY STUFFED ZUCCHINI BOATS

2 large zucchini

½ teaspoon fine sea salt

1 tablespoon extra-virgin olive oil

4 ounces soy chorizo, vegetarian sausage, or meatless crumbles

1 shallot, minced

¾ cup vegetable broth

2 cups dried seasoned stuffing or toasted bread cubes

3 ounces soft goat cheese or feta cheese, crumbled

1 cup baby arugula leaves

¼ cup grated Parmesan cheese

If you're a true carnivore, try this with bulk sausage, making sure it's cooked completely and drained before assembling.

OVEN TEMPERATURE 350°F   **GRILL** MEDIUM HEAT
FOIL 4 SHEETS NONSTICK FOIL OR FOIL LIGHTLY COATED WITH COOKING SPRAY
SIZE 12" X 24"   **TENT-STYLE** PACKAGE   **SERVES** 4

1 Preheat the oven to 350°F or your grill to medium heat.

2 Slice the zucchini in half lengthwise. Scoop the seeds with a small spoon and discard, making a ¼-inch shell. Sprinkle the inside of the zucchini with salt. Turn the squash upside down on paper towels and let drain for 5 to 10 minutes while making the stuffing.

3 Heat the oil in a large skillet over medium heat. Add the soy sausage and shallot and cook, stirring frequently, until browned and crumbly. Add the broth and stuffing, stirring until blended. Add the goat cheese and arugula, stirring until blended.

4 Turn the squash over and place one slice on each piece of foil. Spoon the stuffing mixture evenly into the zucchini shells. Sprinkle each evenly with the Parmesan cheese.

5 Fold the foil over the squash and crimp the edges for tent-style packages. Cook for 35 minutes, until thoroughly heated.

VEGAN TAMALE DUMPLINGS

1 cup vegetable broth

1¼ cups cornmeal

1 (14.5-ounce) can fire-roasted diced tomatoes, drained

½ onion, finely chopped

2 garlic cloves, minced

2 tablespoons chili powder

1 teaspoon ground cumin

2 teaspoons chopped canned chipotle peppers in adobo sauce

½ teaspoon lime zest

1 tablespoon fresh lime juice

1 (15.5-ounce) can pinto beans, rinsed and drained

1 (15.5-ounce) can black beans, rinsed and drained

1 (15.25-ounce) can corn kernels, rinsed and drained, or 1½ cups fresh or frozen

1 cup frozen and thawed vegetarian meat crumbles

While delicious, tamales are very labor intensive and require a bit of skill to work the cornmeal masa on corn husks. This tasty dinner offers all the flavors of tamales while being easily assembled. Make sure there is space in the top of each package, since the steam from the vegetables will cook the tamale dumpling.

OVEN TEMPERATURE 350°F **GRILL** MEDIUM HEAT
FOIL 4 SHEETS NONSTICK FOIL OR FOIL LIGHTLY COATED WITH COOKING SPRAY
SIZE 12" X 18" **TENT-STYLE** PACKAGE **SERVES** 4

---

1 Preheat the oven to 350°F or your grill to medium heat.

2 Combine the vegetable broth and cornmeal in a small bowl. Let stand 10 minutes while preparing the vegetable mixture.

3 Combine the tomatoes, onion, garlic, chili powder, cumin, chipotle peppers, lime zest, lime juice, beans, corn, and meat crumbles in a large bowl.

4 Combine the broth and the cornmeal in a small bowl. Spoon the bean mixture evenly into the center of each piece of foil. Dollop the cornmeal mixture (it will be thin but will firm up when cooked) evenly on the beans.

5 Fold the foil over the mixture and crimp the edges for tent-style packages. Cook for 35 minutes, until the vegetables are hot and the dumplings are cooked through.

VEGGIES AND BARLEY WITH PEANUT SAUCE

Barley is a grain with a chewy texture and a nutty flavor. It needs to be cooked before assembling this dish, since it requires more liquid than the vegetables will provide. Try cooked brown rice, farro, or quinoa as substitutes. For added protein, stir cubed tofu into the peanut sauce before assembling.

OVEN TEMPERATURE 375°F **GRILL** MEDIUM HEAT
FOIL 4 SHEETS NONSTICK FOIL OR
FOIL LIGHTLY COATED WITH COOKING SPRAY
SIZE 12" X 17" **TENT-STYLE** PACKAGE **SERVES** 4

---

2 garlic cloves, coarsely chopped

1 tablespoon minced fresh ginger

2 tablespoons honey

½ cup creamy peanut butter

¼ cup soy or tamari sauce

1 tablespoon fresh lemon juice

1 tablespoon toasted sesame oil

⅛ teaspoon crushed red pepper flakes

1 pound asparagus, cut into 2-inch pieces

2 cups small cauliflower florets

2 cup small broccoli florets

2 carrots, peeled and sliced

1 cup cubed extra-firm or smoked tofu (optional)

2 cups cooked barley

1 Preheat the oven to 375°F or your grill to medium heat.

2 Combine the garlic, ginger, honey, peanut butter, soy sauce, lemon juice, sesame oil, and pepper flakes in a blender. Process until the mixture is smooth, and then transfer to a large bowl. Stir the vegetables and tofu, if using, into the peanut sauce, tossing until coated.

3 Spoon ½ cup of the barley into the center of each foil sheet. Divide the vegetables evenly and place over the barley.

4 Fold the foil over the mixture and crimp the edges for tent-style packages. Cook for 30 minutes, until the vegetables are tender and hot.

METRIC CHARTS

The recipes that appear in this cookbook use the standard US method for measuring liquid and dry or solid ingredients (teaspoons, tablespoons, and cups). The information on these pages is provided to help cooks outside the United States successfully use these recipes. All equivalents are approximate.

METRIC EQUIVALENTS FOR DIFFERENT TYPES OF INGREDIENTS

A standard cup measure of a dry or solid ingredient will vary in weight depending on the type of ingredient. A standard cup of liquid is the same volume for any type of liquid. Use the following chart when converting standard cup measures to grams (weight) or milliliters (volume).

STANDARD CUP	FINE POWDER (ex. flour)	GRAIN (ex. rice)	GRANULAR (ex. sugar)	LIQUID SOLIDS (ex. butter)	LIQUID (ex. milk)
1	140 g	150 g	190 g	200 g	240 ml
¾	105 g	113 g	143 g	150 g	180 ml
⅔	93 g	100 g	125 g	133 g	160 ml
½	70 g	75 g	95 g	100 g	120 ml
⅓	47 g	50 g	63 g	67 g	80 ml
¼	35 g	38 g	48 g	50 g	60 ml
⅛	18 g	19 g	24 g	25g	30 ml

USEFUL EQUIVALENTS FOR DRY INGREDIENTS BY WEIGHT

(To convert ounces to grams, multiply the number of ounces by 30.)

OZ	LB	G
1 oz	¹⁄₁₆ lb	30 g
4 oz	¼ lb	120 g
8 oz	½ lb	240 g
12 oz	¾ lb	360 g
16 oz	1 lb	480 g

USEFUL EQUIVALENTS FOR LENGTH

(To convert inches to centimeters, multiply the number of inches by 2.5.)

IN	FT	YD	CM	M
1 in			2.5 cm	
6 in	½ ft		15 cm	
12 in	1 ft		30 cm	
36 in	3 ft	1 yd	90 cm	
40 in			100 cm	1 m

USEFUL EQUIVALENTS FOR LIQUID INGREDIENTS BY VOLUME

TSP	TBSP	CUPS	FL OZ	ML	L
¼ tsp				1 ml	
½ tsp				2 ml	
1 tsp				5 ml	
3 tsp	1 Tbsp		½ fl oz	15 ml	
	2 Tbsp	⅛ cup	1 fl oz	30 ml	
	4 Tbsp	¼ cup	2 fl oz	60 ml	
	5⅓ Tbsp	⅓ cup	3 fl oz	80 ml	
	8 Tbsp	½ cup	4 fl oz	120 ml	
	10⅔ Tbsp	⅔ cup	5 fl oz	160 ml	
	12 Tbsp	¾ cup	6 fl oz	180 ml	
	16 Tbsp	1 cup	8 fl oz	240 ml	
	1 pt	2 cups	16 fl oz	480 ml	
	1 qt	4 cups	32 fl oz	960 ml	
			33 fl oz	1000 ml	1 l

USEFUL EQUIVALENTS FOR COOKING/OVEN TEMPERATURES

	FAHRENHEIT	CELSIUS	GAS MARK
FREEZE WATER	32° F	0° C	
ROOM TEMPERATURE	68° F	20° C	
BOIL WATER	212° F	100° C	
	325° F	160° C	3
	350° F	180° C	4
	375° F	190° C	5
	400° F	200° C	6
	425° F	220° C	7
	450° F	230° C	8
BROIL		Grill	

INDEX

C

ABOUT THE AUTHOR

×

Julia Rutland is a Washington, DC–area writer and recipe developer whose work appears regularly in publications and websites such as *Southern Living* magazine, *Coastal Living* magazine, and Weight Watchers books. She is the author of *Discover Dinnertime*, *The Campfire Foodie Cookbook*, *On a Stick*, *Blueberries*, and *Squash*. Julia lives in the DC wine country town of Hillsboro, Virginia, with her husband, two daughters, and many furred and feathered friends.